Talk, Listen and Learn

How to boost your child's language and learning ability

Linda Clark & Catherine Ireland

HarperCollins*Publishers*

HarperCollins*Publishers*

First published in Australia by Bay Books in 1994 as *Learning to Talk, Talking to Learn*
The Angus and Robertson edition published in 1996
This edition published in 2003
by HarperCollins*Publishers* Pty Limited
ABN 36 009 913 517
A member of the HarperCollins*Publishers* (Australia) Pty Limited Group
www.harpercollins.com.au

HarperCollins*Publishers*
25 Ryde Road, Pymble, Sydney, NSW 2073, Australia
31 View Road, Glenfield, Auckland 10, New Zealand
77-85 Fulham Palace Road, London W6 8JB, United Kingdom
2 Bloor Street East, 20th floor, Toronto, Ontario M4W 1A8, Canada
10 East 53rd Street, New York NY 10022, USA

National Library of Australia Cataloguing-in-Publication data:

Clark, Linda.
  Talk, listen and learn: how to boost your child's language
  and learning ability.
  Bibliography.
  Includes index.
  ISBN 0 7322 7522 9.
  1. Children – Language. 2. Language arts (Primary).
  I. Ireland, Catherine. II. Clark, Linda. Learning to talk,
  talking to learn. III. Title.
372.6

Cover photograph: The Photo Library/Mario Krmpotic
Photography: Petrina Tinslay
Cover design: Judi Rowe
Internal design by Louise McGeachie
Set in 12/16 Sabon
Printed and bound in Australia by Griffin Press on 70gsm Ensobelle

6 5 4 3 2 1   03 04 05 06

Linda Clark qualified as a Speech and Language Therapist in London and has worked in England, Australia, Singapore and Indonesia. She is currently working in private practice in Adelaide, South Australia. Linda's work in expatriate schools in Asia enabled her to participate in the sharing of knowledge and experiences with professionals and children from all over the world.

Catherine Ireland qualified as a Speech Pathologist in Brisbane, Queensland and has worked in Canada and Australia. She is currently employed by the Department of Education and Children's Services in Adelaide, South Australia. Catherine's work with parents and teachers has highlighted the need for early intervention, support and guidance for children with speech and language problems.

Dedication

We are indebted to all those parents and children we have worked with who have shared their skills with us. Not least we must thank our own children — James, Sarah, Whitney and Kate — who have allowed us to experience child development and parenting first-hand. At the same time we would like to thank those in our families who supported us through so many of our own learning experiences.

Best wishes to all the children we have worked with over the years. Good luck to them in whichever country they live and whatever they are doing.

Preface

Linda Clark and Catherine Ireland are speech pathologists combining over fifty years' experience helping children with speech, language and literacy problems. Speech pathology services are in great demand, many of which have long waiting lists.

When Linda and Catherine first qualified as speech pathologists the children referred to them were generally well into their primary schooling. Thankfully, increased community awareness in recent years meant children are being referred at a much earlier stage. Nevertheless, today, many parents expressing concern over their children's speech and language development are often advised to 'wait and see' by other professionals and friends.

Over the years many people approached Linda and Catherine seeking guidance to mitigate or eliminate speech difficulties in their children or other family members. As a response, they ran a series of small hands-on workshops in 1992 for groups of parents and new babies. During this time they were continually asked if there was a text to accompany the workshops. They concluded that a book was likely to reach a far wider audience of parents and professionals, and this resulted in the first edition of *Learning to Talk, Talking to Learn* in 1994.

Feedback from this edition was positive: mainly that the book provided useful information for parents with children from birth to four years. However, there was little or no literature that supported children's language development skills beyond the age of four years.

Hence the aim of this new edition, *Talk, Listen and Learn*, is to provide guidance for children from birth through to ten years, including significant additional information on literacy and the use of technology.

The authors hope that their book will offer parents and professionals the knowledge and confidence to seek early guidance and support for children with speech, language and literacy problems. By doing so, many more children will secure the best available start in life.

Foreword

Early speech and language development will stand your child in good stead for the rest of his life. The ideas in this book can help make the first few years of your child's life fun for both you and your child. You will see how important it is to talk to him, play with him, read with him and show him that you love him. Try to be enthusiastic! If you praise his early successes, he will be more likely to want to repeat activities and learn more.

We hope this book will help you discover the many natural talents you have as parents and carers, which you can use with your child every day. By combining these talents with the ideas provided in *Talk, Listen and Learn*, you can be confident of giving your child the kind of stimulation he needs to develop his language and learning abilities to full advantage.

For ease of reading and understanding, the word 'he' has been used to refer to both male and female children. Speech pathologists are commonly known as 'therapists' and will sometimes be referred to as such throughout this book.

Contents

Introduction

Most of us take learning to talk for granted, yet all parents know the thrill — and the wonderful sense of achievement — when our children begin to talk to us.

Speech and language provides the foundation for developing academic and social skills. Language refers to all the different ways we communicate, including not only the way we talk but the way we listen, gesture, read and write.

To understand the world around them, children must have names for people, things and actions. They need to reason why and when things happen and even to manipulate people and events.

Studies of language development have shown beyond doubt that early development of speech is the one skill that will stand children in good stead for the rest of their lives; early sitting, walking or first teeth, on the other hand, do not have any relevance to later academic ability. While late talkers do not always have problems in the classroom, it is very rare for early skilled talkers to have learning difficulties.

As parents, most of us do things as a matter of course to help our children learn to talk. However, without an understanding of how language develops we can sometimes put obstacles in the way or not take advantage of certain situations.

The aim of this book is to give you the information, ideas, activities and skills required to boost your child's language and learning abilities. It is not aimed at creating a 'genius' or turning you into a formal teacher, but at helping you make the most of your child's enormous potential.

Talk, Listen and Learn is for all parents and carers who want to help young children — especially in their first ten years — learn to talk and talk better or earlier than they might otherwise. It will show you how to:

- teach your child to talk, in a relaxed and practical way;
- expand your child's speech and language skills by always keeping one step ahead;
- expand your child's vocabulary and general knowledge;
- encourage your child to want to learn;
- expand your child's learning potential;
- make communication easier;
- make communication more fun for your child and your family;
- enjoy your child more as he develops.

As speech pathologists we have worked for a number of years with children who have problems with speech and language development, including those:

- who are late in speaking;
- whose speech is unclear;
- who are dysfluent or who stutter;
- who have difficulty understanding what is said to them;
- who have problems with their grammar and vocabulary.

Drawing on our experience as speech pathologists and as parents, we will show you how you can use everyday situations and relaxed, happy playtime to help your child learn to talk. In doing this you can help prevent some speech and language problems, increase your child's learning potential and enjoy your child.

1 **Talking to learn**

Communication skills are arguably the most important skills we can gain in life. The nature of our communication skills will affect our relationships, education, employment opportunities — every aspect of our lives.

Our views of people are often based on our first impressions of the way they look and speak. We have found that teachers often use a child's verbal skills as a measure of his abilities. Whether we like it or not, a child may be labelled 'slow' or 'bright' because of the way he talks.

Think about how you communicate. You need to listen, take turns, understand what is said to you, create your own ideas, and have the vocabulary and grammar to express yourself. Even the sequence of your sounds, words and ideas is important. Your child, too, needs to learn all this just to talk.

Following are some of the vital things children are learning to do as they develop into special little individuals. You'll see how talking plays an integral part in each of them.

Asking for things he wants

We see many young children who are unable to ask for a drink or a toy. They resort to pointing, pulling and screaming to try to tell their parents what they want. The poor parent can only try to guess. Both parents and child end up feeling exhausted and frustrated. How much easier it would be if he could say 'Drink please.'

Seeking information to learn about new things

As parents we have all been worn down by the two-year-old with the constant 'What's that?' or the three- or four-year-old asking 'Why?' But this is their way of finding out what things are and how things happen. Likewise, playing with a toy that requires a child to do something in order for it to work encourages him to have a more inquiring mind.

Talking about experiences, feelings and things about himself

By talking about their likes, fears and moods, children learn to deal with their feelings and emotions. Once the child has verbalised such feelings we can provide appropriate support and aim to increase his emotional security.

Young children love to give their opinions on all sorts of subjects. One of our children has always been very quick to offer an opinion on her mother's clothes: 'Mum, that colour just doesn't look good on you. I like the blue jumper better.' Dare we say, she is often right! This form of language reflects your child's personality, showing preferences and an interest or lack of it.

Talking to themselves about what they are doing or what they are going to do can also encourage children to express feelings and emotions more openly. Thinking aloud is another way young children begin to express more about themselves.

Developing social skills including making friends and enlisting the help of others

The way we use our talking can influence the way others respond to us. If you said to your spouse 'Get me a newspaper', their response would probably be 'Go and get it yourself.' This doesn't help the relationship. A more tactful and polite approach may have got you the newspaper.

A child can learn how to use his talking more effectively. Learning how to greet friends is important: a 'Hey! You!' shouted across the kindergarten playground may not entice peers to join in with your child's play.

Having a friend join in is not the only objective; a child must also learn to use his language to gain his turn, offer to share, take turns in conversation and play cooperatively.

Young children can also learn to make jokes and tease appropriately as well as how to sympathise: 'Oh no. Is your finger hurting? I'll go and ask the teacher for a Band-aid.'

Enjoying using language to create an imaginary world

The 'let's make believe' world of children provides a safe environment for them to try out different ways of communicating. Playing 'mummies and daddies' or 'schools' enables the child to experience different roles, such as being boss or being naughty.

While an active imagination is sometimes frowned upon, life would be very boring without the new ideas and inventions that such imaginations produce.

Making his own decisions and thinking independently

Teaching our children to make decisions and solve problems helps develop their ability to think independently. As parents we can provide problem-solving practice in everyday routines. We can discuss alternative solutions and resolve the problem out loud: 'What would you like for dessert? Peter is having fruit but you can have fruit or ice cream.'

Life is full of situations where the rules are inappropriate. As parents we often ask our children to do things, expecting them not to take us literally but to apply their own judgment to the situation.

We were once at a friend's place when the mother and her daughter were making toast for lunch. The telephone rang and the mother called to her daughter to watch the toast. She did just as she was told and watched the toast burn and catch alight. Unfortunately the daughter did not make an independent decision.

There may be times where taking the initiative may be crucial to a child's safety. If told 'never speak to strangers', a child may be afraid to seek help in dangerous situations.

Taking important steps towards reading

If a child's talking is limited and unclear it may be much harder for him to make sense of the written word. If we think of the written word as an extension of talking, then reading will clearly be easier for a child with good verbal skills.

2 **Learning to talk from you**

Learning to talk doesn't begin with the child's first words but long before that — from the time of birth and even before. Babies have a built-in interest in listening to voices and will start to grasp language long before they can use it themselves. This is the first thing to appreciate in helping a child learn to talk: understanding is always one step ahead of talking. Becoming familiar with more complex words and sentences is how we all learnt to eventually use them ourselves.

Think about people learning a foreign language. It is generally accepted that their understanding is about six months ahead of their speech. If you apply that rule-of-thumb to children, and take account of the vast amount they learn in six months at this steep part of life's learning curve, you will begin to see just how much we may not give them credit for!

Learning to talk, then, is largely dependent on being stimulated with words and sentences of ever-increasing complexity. The bulk of this stimulation comes from a child's parents and other regular carers.

So how do we stimulate a child in this way? Do we just talk all the time? Talking to babies who can't answer back is easier for some people than for others who feel very self-conscious. And anyway, is this really all we have to do?

Fortunately, parents are natural teachers and, equipped with a basic understanding of how children learn to talk, you can provide just the right type of stimulation at each stage of your child's development.

Certainly, this stimulation is not just a matter of 'any talking will do'. Dr Paula Menyuk, Director of the Language Behavior Program at Boston University's School of Education, studied communication in 56 families with young children. She reported that language skills were better developed in the children whose parents spoke to them directly and allowed them time to respond than in those whose parents simply talked all the time. Menyuk showed that it is possible for parents to overstimulate so that there is no noticeable benefit to their child's language development. The child appears to 'switch off' to constant chatter, which becomes background noise rather like television can be. More structured conversation, on the other hand, was shown to benefit the child's language growth substantially.

'Structured conversation' might sound formal, but it doesn't mean you have to sit down and have a speech lesson. Everyday activities provide the best experiences for language development. Get into the habit of telling your child all the things you are doing, what you are using and what comes next. Talk while you are sweeping the floor. Show your toddler the 'broom', let him try pushing it 'up' and 'down'.

Everyday activities provide all the opportunities you need for dialogue, questions and answers, and carrying out commands, as well as giving you appropriate settings in which to name objects:

'Look, John. Look, a potato. It's a big potato. Hold the potato. Shall I cut it? I'll cut up the potato and put it into the saucepan. Look at the potato.'

This helps your child learn talking is about things, and things have names which are useful.

Try to avoid constant background and other noise when you're encouraging your child to talk. It is hard for him to pay attention to you with television and other noises in the same room. If you are aware of this, you can minimise the effect.

Listen carefully to your child and try to answer every time he 'talks' to you. You don't need to stop what you're doing every time he makes a noise, but speech will increase if your child believes that talking gets results.

Make every effort to understand him when you see that he's trying to communicate. If he doesn't have the words to explain, ask if he can show you what he means.

Communication skills

Communication is the sharing of information, desires and ideas. It is a two-way interaction: both the speaker and the listener need to be able to send, receive and understand messages in order to communicate effectively. Talking is only one way of communicating a message: other means include gesturing, reading and writing. In order to communicate by talking, a child needs to learn competence in a number of areas: language, comprehension, articulation, expression, sequencing, listening and intonation.

Language is the system of rules which governs the words we use. English has hundreds of rules, which our children need to learn. For example, we add an '-s' for plurals and use '-is' with '-ing' endings when talking about the present, as in 'he is sitting'. There are also many exceptions to the rules!

Comprehension refers to the understanding of language and is also known as receptive language. Verbal comprehension is when a child can relate a spoken word to a meaningful object in any form or context. He will learn that a word can represent an action, object or thought. By listening to you talk as you go about your daily routines, your child will start to associate the words with the action, the object or the thought you describe. For example, he would learn when you say the word 'cup' he knows you are referring to the object with a handle from which he drinks. Before you can say any words, you need to be able to understand what the words mean. There is an exception to this rule in the case of a child with a language disorder, which will be discussed in a later chapter.

Articulation is the use of the tongue, lips, teeth and palate to form speech sounds. These sounds develop from birth to seven years.

Things to teach your child about talking

Talking is a two-way activity
— this makes it good fun!
Talking has a purpose
— it explains things and directs activity.
Talking gets results
— he can use it to get what he wants ...
sometimes!

Expression (or expressive language) is the way we convey an idea using a combination of words, intonation and body language. We use body language and intonation all the time to enhance our communication interactions and help give meaning to the words spoken: you may talk about a *blackbird* or a *black bird*, and you certainly wouldn't expect much response from your child if you told him off using a gentle tone of voice and with a smile on your face. All of our body movements convey a meaning whether we like it or not and mostly we do it unconsciously. The way we stand, sit, lean, breathe and look conveys meaning to our audience.

Sequencing is being able to put sounds, words and eventually ideas into the correct order for the listener to understand. For example with sounds, the four-legged furry animal which meows is a c-a-t not

HOW COMMUNICATION DEVELOPS

0 to 3 months Cries, makes eye contact, smiles. Responds to sounds.

3 to 6 months Makes a variety of noises that sound more like speech. Also uses a range of non-speech sounds such as squealing and yelling. Recognises the difference between angry and friendly voices.

6 to 12 months Recognises common objects by name. Uses simple gestures like clapping hands, shouts to attract attention. Babbling becomes more complex. Begins to use facial expression (such as eye gazing), vocalisation and gestures (reaching, pointing) to communicate.

12 to 18 months Starts to use lots of single words, although they may not be clearly spoken.

18 months to 2 years Understands a lot of what is said to him. Starts using little sentences.

2 to 3 years Quantity of speech greatly increases. Talks about events in the 'here and now'. Becoming quite skilled at conversation. Takes turns speaking and listening. Responds to directions and questions. By three years, strangers should understand your child most of the time, although errors are still made with sounds.

3 to 5 years Makes sentences and tells stories. Has a very large vocabulary and can use sentences of eight or more words. Can relay information. Can talk about events that happened yesterday or will happen tomorrow. Constantly asks questions.

5 to 7 years Your child talks almost as well as you. All sounds are produced clearly. Occasional errors are made with irregular verbs ('broked' instead of 'broken'). Vocabulary continues to expand.

an a-c-t or a t-a-c. Regarding words, imagine the listener's reaction if you said 'Table the on hat is the'. Similarly with ideas, it would be confusing to tell the story: 'He was thrown off when he hit a stone. The boy was riding his bike. His leg is in plaster. He was rushed to hospital.' Our sounds, words and ideas need to be sequenced to convey information. Like writing a story, we use a beginning, a middle and an end.

Listening is paying attention to the sounds you hear so you can interpret their meaning. In order to be able to understand (or have good verbal comprehension), your child must be able to listen well. He needs to be able to interpret the sounds he hears in a word so he can understand the meaning. This is different from hearing, which is an automatic physical response to a stimulus. We all know children (and indeed some adults!) who have nothing physically wrong with their hearing but who don't seem to listen.

Intonation is the 'music' in your voice, the way it goes up and down and stresses certain syllables. Intonation can change the meaning of a word. For example, by changing intonation we can say 'yes' to mean 'definitely yes', 'maybe', 'if I have to' or 'who is it?'

With his careful attention to your tone of voice and your movements, your baby is already learning about talking.

BABBLING

Your baby starts crying from the moment he is born; this is his only means of communicating. Although all you may hear is crying and feel it all sounds the same, in fact, your newborn is building up a repertoire of different cries to express his needs and feelings. You will soon learn to distinguish his different cries and you may be surprised to see how quickly you respond to a cry suggesting pain as opposed to a cry suggesting he has just awoken from a nap. You will also find once you interpret his cry, you will then tell your baby what you think he means. This way you are teaching him to establish a link between spoken language and his body language. For example, as you lift him out of his cot because you think he is in pain say to him 'Oh darling, you got your finger stuck. Is that why you are crying?'

Learning to communicate, however, does not just begin when the baby is born, but rather at the start of life in the womb. Babies have had nine months' practice listening to their mother's voice, so it is not surprising they can distinguish between men's and women's voices within the first few weeks of life, and show a preference for their own mother's voice over other female voices. Lots of mothers would have experienced their baby's different responses to sounds during their pregnancy. Once a baby is born you will notice that loud, sudden sounds will make his body jump, while he will often show his pleasure at a regular rhythmical voice. When you are holding your baby and paying close attention, you will notice he will listen more attentively to voices even though he hears lots of sounds. If he is lying still when you begin to speak, his body will start to move excitedly. By about three months, he has even sorted out the difference between smiling and talking, so he smiles back at smiles and talks back at speech. It is important even at this stage to talk directly to your baby as often as you can, because research has shown toddlers will have a larger vocabulary if their parents speak to them a lot when they are babies. They are likely to be more talkative children, while those who are handled in silence will be less talkative. This has implications for their social interactions and other learning experiences.

Turn-taking

You can spend many happy hours with your baby cooing and gurgling together, taking turns listening and making sounds. This enjoyable game is important for language learning as it practises the turn-taking of conversation which your baby will need later on. When we interact this way with a baby, we are turning anything the baby does into a form of communication. When the baby startles we may say 'Wow, that's a big noise', or when baby coughs and splutters we may say 'Oh, that was a big cough. Mummy's got you.' It's as if you are giving him a turn to 'talk' and though he doesn't know it now, you are teaching him the basics of conversational turn-taking. Remember communication is about turn-taking. Most of us don't enjoy a one-sided conversation!

There are several ways we can play with a baby to teach him about turn-taking. Hold your face close to his so you have a better chance of holding his attention. Close physical contact promotes this and, if you think about it, most adults hold babies very close to their faces in the first few months of life, which is just as well because babies can only focus on objects that are about half-an-arm's-length away. Play a game or sing a song in a fun way over and over. The more familiar he is with the words, the more he will want to 'join in' and take a turn. Practice also lets him anticipate the right time to 'join in'. If you are babbling to him, pause and give him a chance to 'tell' you to do it again. He will gradually learn that whatever he does to respond will get you to do it again; this is his way of taking turns and having an effect on your behaviour. It is also teaching him about cause and effect: if I laugh she will laugh back to me! Lots of toys we use with infants teach them this skill: if I push the button the clown will pop his head out!

Just as voices are the most important things to listen to, so are faces the most important thing to look at. Speak directly to your baby from a close distance and see how he watches the movement of your lips. With his careful attention to your tone of voice and your movements, your baby is already learning a lot about talking.

Of course, babies don't only speak when spoken to, they will chatter away to themselves for hours in their cots and prams. Although you can't understand a word of it, you will notice how your baby maintains the conversational rhythm: he makes sounds then pauses as if to listen, and then 'responds'. Talk to babies as if they can talk to you.

Babbling sounds take form

Between **four and six months**, your baby is becoming more physically able and this enables him to express himself with body language in a more sophisticated way. He may be crying less but the crying is more specific in its meaning. There's less guesswork for us.

HOW TO HAVE GREAT FUN CHANGING NAPPIES

Daily chores are a great chance to help your child learn to talk and they can be made more fun with a little bit of imagination. Be relaxed with your child. Chat with him and enjoy his company — even if you are changing his nappy for the tenth time that day!

Here are some ideas for a speech lesson on the change table:

- Have a bright picture on the wall at your child's eye level, or a noisy toy. Draw his attention to it and tell him its name.
- Talk about the cloth you're using. 'Does it tickle your leg? Now I'm rubbing it on your arm.'
- Tickle his feet with the lotion bottle while you tell him what it is.
- Encourage him to copy you by blowing raspberries, poking out his tongue or making cooing sounds.
- Play peek-a-boo with a nappy, or hide a toy under the nappy.

By about **six months** he will start linking streams of his sounds together to 'babble'. With practice, his babbling becomes more and more complicated — talk to your baby to help him expand his range of sounds.

The babbling sounds used by babies seem to be universal, and even deaf babies who cannot hear use these sounds until about six months. Experts believe that after this age, infants tend to only pay attention to the everyday sounds that he hears that belong to his language. The usual babbling sounds are 'ba', 'ka', 'ma', 'da', 'pa'. This is a wonderful age as we watch our baby make raspberries and laugh out loud.

While babbling does not influence the age at which first words are used, it does help babies practise sound combinations, so babbling to your baby is actually serving a very important purpose, as well as being fun.

Don't panic if your baby doesn't babble. While most children do, there are others who don't say anything until they utter their first word and they go on to have adequate speech and language skills.

Mimicking and repeating words

By about **eight months** most babies have started to take greater interest in adult conversation, even when it is not directed at them. When sitting between two adults, your baby might turn his head, as if at a tennis match, as each person speaks. But he won't be left out for long. Soon he will contribute his own chatter to the conversation or let out a shout to regain attention. At this stage, his speech is beginning to mimic the inflection of adult conversation; you will notice it often sounds like he is asking a question. Include him in your conversations, listen to his babbling and when he pauses in anticipation, respond with an 'answer'.

Watch your baby closely and remember all his pointing, eye gazing and crying have meaning too. If he pushes, points or throws something, he will wait for a response from you. This is showing you he is starting to understand the relationship between receptive and expressive language. You can encourage him to communicate more by showing you understand what he wants or feels and by showing there are words to describe these things.

Remember that the understanding of speech develops prior to talking. Your child cannot learn to ask for an object unless he knows what it is called. From as early as **six to nine months** you can start repeating common words in a way that will teach your baby the association between the sound and the object or action. Use short sentences and pause frequently:

'Look at the onion. Mmmmm, smell the onion. I'll take the skin off. Now I'll chop the onion.'

This technique is discussed at some length in the section, 'Language takes off'.

Although he's not using real words yet, he may use the same sounds each time he wants to convey the same message. He might say 'buhbuhbuh' each time he wants to be picked up or he may look down to the floor every time you say your pet's name. He is showing you he understands the meaning of the pet's name and knows the pet is always down below his level on the floor.

Continue to encourage his listening skills. When you hear an everyday sound such as a telephone or the bath water running, ask your child what it is and find the source of the sound together.

All of this will guide your baby towards uttering his first words.

FIRST WORDS

By about **ten to 12 months**, many children will say their first word. Parents are so delighted they try to get the child to say it over and over. Children need lots and lots of praise to make them feel it is worthwhile continuing to learn to say more words. First words are usually the names of people, animals or objects that are of interest to your child, as well as useful words like 'more' and 'up'.

When you feel your child is getting ready to make his first attempts at meaningful speech, it can be helpful to choose half-a-dozen words and concentrate on these. Words that can be used often such as 'daddy' and 'milk' will get the best results. A study by Macquarie University in 1988 found that children use a wide variety of words when they first start talking. The table on page 18 includes the most frequently used first words. This will also give you an idea of the range of words you can encourage.

Relevance and repetition

Relevance and repetition are very important at this stage. We all find it easier to learn new things that mean something to us, so there is no point in teaching your infant the word 'dog' if he is scared of dogs. You need to show your child what the word means and to say it for him repeatedly. For example, when he holds out his cup for more juice, ask 'More? More?' and then pause. Then pour him more juice and explain: 'More'. Eventually he will imitate your word when you pause for his response.

Similarly, when you go to pick him up from the floor you might ask 'Up?' and then pause. When you pick him up, you exclaim 'Up!' in an exaggerated voice. He will begin to realise that when he wants you to get him off the floor, the relevant word is 'up'. Note how in both examples, we have stressed the idea of pausing after you've spoken;

this is again teaching him the skill of turn-taking and letting him know that it does take two to talk.

Simple games such as 'clap hands' are also useful at this stage. Your child will learn that when you say both those words, you are describing the action of putting his hands together. Just as you would show your child the relevant object when you are teaching him a word, so too do you show him the action that you are describing so he learns that doing things have names too.

Once your child shows an interest in learning to talk, try to keep your conversations with him as simple as possible. It is very confusing to the child if every object is named but each name is only mentioned once. Similarly, if the words form a long complex sentence, he can lose the meaning altogether. For example, it is much easier to learn the meaning of 'more' in the situation described above than from a question such as 'Would you like some more juice to drink darling?' Given our aim at this stage is to encourage him to listen and talk, there is no point in making it as hard as possible for him. It will be a much more rewarding experience for you and your child if he can understand what you say to him.

A child's first real words are often difficult to identify. Listen carefully to your child's babbling and see whether he uses a sound consistently: is he trying to say a word? Children learning to talk often think that any word will do and insistently use their own words, for instance 'bop' might mean 'milk'. If he uses it consistently then you should accept it as his own word for that object. If you start saying 'No, it's not bop' he may become confused. You need to keep your child motivated and let him know he is doing well. Gradually over time, you can provide the correct model for him by saying 'You want milk?' after he has said 'bop'. You must remember he will probably point to the carton of milk as he says 'bop' so usually parents can understand what he is saying by interpreting his gesture as well as his 'word'.

Children of this age can be very persistent in getting their message across. If, for example, he wants a favourite teddy from the floor he may point and look at the teddy, look at you, look at the object again

ACTIVITIES TO ENCOURAGE FIRST WORDS

- Listen for everyday sounds and ask your child 'What's that?' Encourage your child to listen carefully and to guess what is making the sound. Then track it down and discover the source of the sound.

- Stand toys, one at a time, on the lid of a box. When your child is watching make the toys fall into the box and exclaim 'Gone!'

- When playing with blocks, make the most of opportunities to use words like 'up', 'more' and 'all fall down'.

- Have a tea party with all the dolls and teddies. Offer each toy a drink or biscuit with the same repetitive questions: 'More drink?', 'More biscuit?'

- Find and name parts of the body, with or without rhymes. Make it more difficult by asking your child to find 'your eyes' and 'my eyes'.

- Use often-repeated phrases with exaggerated intonation: 'Where are you?' when looking for any person or object.

- Don't forget to name actions as well as objects: 'Come and eat'.

- Provide words to express feelings and to get help. Draw pictures of teddies looking sad, cross, happy and surprised.

- Show your child how to blow bubbles. It is actually quite difficult for young children, but good practice for later speech production. It also provides an opportunity to teach words like 'more', 'bubbles', 'pop' and 'gone'.

- Hold your baby's hand and wave goodbye from as young as two or three months.

and make a sound, then look at you again. He might even say 'Ted', as if to say 'Can't you see I want my teddy?'

At this stage offering him choices can boost your child's language.

FIRST WORDS

People	Objects	Location words	Actions	Modifiers	Socially useful
Mummy	apple	up	kiss	more	bye-bye
Daddy	ball	down	sleep	my	hi
Baby	bikky	there	gimme	your	hello
Family names	bus	here	want	big	no
....	car	in	wash	little	please
....	cup	on	eat	mine	thanks
....	comb	that	drink	hot	to
Child's name	dolly		down	that	
Teacher's name	shoe		fall	this	
....	spoon		comb/brush	a	
....	sweets		gone/all gone	yuk!	
....	teddy		go		
	bath		stop		
Names of pets	man		throw		
....	bed		up		
....	eye		in		
	key		do		
Favourite toys	door		open		
....	dog		fix		
....	sock		come		
	TV		look		
Pronouns	book				
Me	light				
I	tree				
You	see-saw				
Mine	clock				

Source: Bochner, S., Price, P. and Salaman, L. *Learning to Talk*, Bochnor, 1988.

It is an excellent way of teaching the child to communicate without putting too much pressure on him. It also helps his understanding. If you are unsure what he wants to play with, hold two choices in front of him. As you show him the objects name them: 'Do you want puzzle (*pause*) or book?' This will make it easier for him to express himself because sometimes it's hard for early talkers to think of the right word at the right time. It will also let him know he has some rights in expressing his preferences. This is also a common technique used with children who are language-delayed.

A child at this stage will often substitute easier sounds for more difficult ones, for example, he might say 'doo' for 'shoe'. He might also leave out sounds at the beginning or end of words, for example, he might say 'cu' for 'cup'. Don't be upset by this. It is better to build his confidence than to discourage him by correcting him all the time. It is far more worthwhile to model the correct pronunciations by exaggerating the altered or missing sound — you make your point and give positive reinforcement for talking, 'Yes, it's a cu*p*' or 'sh_oe'.

Building a word list

Once your child starts talking it is worth keeping a list of the words he can say. You may be very surprised as to how many there are. We have seen children whose parents tell us they can't say any more than two or three words. Once you start playing with the child and pointing out word attempts to parents, they are surprised and say 'Oh, I forgot he said that' and 'Oh, yes, he said that the other day.' So, it is worth keeping a list.

Even though your child's understanding of words is expanding rapidly, you will notice that his meaning is not always the same as the adult meaning of a word. 'Dog' may be any four-legged animal, or he might think a 'ball' is only his round red object he kicks as opposed to the small tennis ball his dog chases.

As your child shows more and more interest in words, keep focusing on objects he finds useful or interesting. Don't worry if a word seems difficult. It will be harder getting him to say 'ball' if all he is interested in is a toy dinosaur. Who cares how he pronounces it at first!

When your child can use some words, you can set up situations where he can practise them. If he's saying 'hat', devise a game using different hats. Keeping in mind that understanding precedes talking, such situations are also a good time to introduce more complexity in the form of qualifying words. When your child says 'hat', say 'Yes, big hat' or 'Yes, Peter's hat.'

As part of using words appropriately, your child will also learn to use his tone of voice to convey different meanings. It is up to the listener to interpret the meaning! When he says 'Daddy', he might mean:

Come here, Daddy!
Where's Daddy?
There's Daddy.
Great! Here's Daddy!
Don't, Daddy!

LANGUAGE TAKES OFF

Once your child has a vocabulary of about 30 words he will be able to start putting words together into two-word sentences. The two-word sentence may be simplistic but it is of great significance because it shows the child's desire — and ability — to communicate an original idea rather than just imitate adults. Words in these first sentences are usually sequenced in the correct order, but there will be words 'missing' compared with more sophisticated sentences. To understand what your child means, therefore, you often have to know the situation. When he says 'Daddy car', does he mean:

That's Daddy's car.
Let's go in Daddy's car.
Is that Daddy's car?
Daddy's gone in the car.

It may come as a surprise to see how much your child has already learnt about language: in the above example, the possessive noun (Daddy) correctly precedes the noun which is owned (car).

Children are great copiers, and this skill is invaluable as your child

HOW TO ENCOURAGE YOUR CHILD TO TALK

- Talk to him about anything — people, things, activities.

- Be animated and vary your voice and facial expressions.

- Show him what you are talking about.

- Take turns.

- Use short, simple, clear sentences to label and expand his world.

- Let him see your face when you are talking.

- Repeat a lot.

- Let him initiate communication.

- Allow him time to talk.

- Read him books and magazines.

- Copy his sounds, as if having a conversation.

- Make it fun!

learns more about talking. By using clear, short and easily understood sentences, you will provide a good model for sentence formation. Keep the speed steady and try not to lapse into fast chatter.

As we've already noted, a child's early sentences often sound like text messages, with little words and grammatical markers omitted, as in 'ball in box'. Techniques for showing him how to fill in the gaps are explained later in this section.

Remember, it takes two to talk

The importance of turn-taking, now that your toddler is developing words, is still significant in helping him learn to communicate.

Just as you did right from the beginning when communicating with your baby, try to convey the message you expect a response. Ask simple questions and pause for an answer. If there is no attempt to talk, repeat the question and after a short pause answer your own question simply:

> *'What do you want?* (pause)
> *What do you want?* (pause)
> *Do you want more juice?* (pause) *More?'*

When your child is talking, it is important you pay attention; after all, you expect him to listen when you are talking. If you are busy talking all the time without giving him time to contribute, when will your child have the opportunity to practise his talking?

Create situations where your child can learn to take his turn. Helping with household chores and playing together are both good opportunities for your child to learn about turn-taking. Take turns stirring the cake or rolling the ball. At first your child may need to be prompted to take his turn.

Encourage eye contact when talking. You don't have to stare into each other's eyes! But looking at the person you are speaking to provides a positive communication environment and is an important skill to learn. Have you ever tried talking to someone who is constantly looking around them? Not only is it very disconcerting, but they seem to be indicating to you they are not interested. That may be true, but it's more likely they are not good at making eye contact.

When communicating is pleasurable for everyone concerned, frequency of speech will increase. You will have experienced this yourself. Everyone speaks more in a relaxed environment, with people they feel comfortable with. When your young child 'talks' back to you, cuddle and praise him for his communication. The tone of your voice and gleam in your eye will make him smile with pleasure.

When your child attempts any sort of talking, respond immediately, even if it's not very convenient. (You can always call from the top of the ladder!) Knowing speech gets action from an adult is very satisfying. At the very least, praise the attempt: 'Good boy. Good talking. You want more.'

What about 'baby talk'?

Grandparents seem particularly fond of baby terms like 'dickie birds' and 'night nights'. Some parents feel baby talk should be limited to the first nine months of life. Indeed, we would suggest there is no need to use baby talk at all. There seems little point or benefit in teaching words which have to be changed at a later date. This can be extremely difficult, especially for children with language problems.

Don't be put off by words which appear hard to say. 'Thank you' may come out as 'tang oo', but your intonation will be imitated as well and this will help you understand.

Your intonation, in fact, is very important. Many people naturally exaggerate their tone of voice and increase the use of facial expression and hand movements when they're talking to young children. If you are enthusiastic and entertaining, you will tend to hold your child's interest much longer. Don't be afraid to exaggerate tonal and physical gestures when interacting with your child: 'Where are you?' with a rise and fall in intonation and 'Thank you' with a fall in intonation.

Quite often intonation is learnt well before the words are mastered. Even though the words are impossible to understand in isolation, you will know from the tone 'Air ar oo?' means 'Where are you?'

Words spoken in an interesting manner are often learnt very quickly. It is not unusual for us to see children whose speech is generally unintelligible but who can articulate 'Oh shit!' as clearly as can be!

Asking questions all the time

Once your child can produce a simple sentence, he will see the value of communication and will rapidly learn more about using his language skills.

Language and knowledge are intimately mixed. His language will enable him to seek information, and this in turn will increase his language ability. A child will need language for his developing thoughts and this need will advance his talking. The more thinking he is doing, the more language he will develop. A child who is helped to use language well will use his potential for learning to good effect. His talking feeds his intelligence.

At **about 18 months of age,** parents notice their children are saying new words every day. They start to ask questions such as 'What's that?' and will use their words to comment on what is happening. They not only use many nouns (names of objects) now, but they are beginning to use other word groups such as verbs (action words such as 'go') and adjectives (describing words such as 'big'). The sooner your child learns a variety of words, rather than just nouns, the sooner he will be able to join more words together.

Body language continues to develop and play an important role. Tantrums are often frequent at this age because of both frustration with performing tasks and the desire to be more independent. Therefore, more exaggerated body language accompanies strong emotional reactions.

This rapid growth in their talking is also accompanied by a daily growth in their understanding of language. Although a child may only be saying about 50 words at this stage, he probably understands about 300 words! He wants to hear the same stories over and over and he can now follow instructions such as 'Go to your room and bring me your shoes.' He can also point to some of his body parts.

Awareness of language and expression

Following are four very useful techniques you can apply at this stage to increase your child's understanding and expression. These strategies are extremely valuable for all age groups.

Self-talk can be used with any activity and refers to the technique whereby you, the adult, talk out loud about what you can see, feel, hear and touch. In other words, as you talk you are describing what you are doing. It is like an ongoing commentary. An example might be: 'I need to find the car keys so we can go out' or 'I'm going to peel an apple for us to eat.'

Parallel talk can also be used in any activity. This time, instead of talking about you, you talk out loud about what your child is seeing, feeling, hearing and touching. Examples include: 'You are drinking your milk' or 'You are patting the cat gently.'

Modelling is really what we do all the time. This is where you revise and complete your child's utterance. For example, if your child says 'dog run', you could reply by modelling 'Yes, the dog is running.' A good speech model is one who keeps a step ahead of the child's level; you don't talk at an adult level and you don't use 'baby talk', you talk just above your child's level.

Expansion refers to the process whereby you add new information to the child's existing language. You don't change the meaning of your child's utterance, but rather repeat what he said and make it longer by adding some more relevant words. For example, if your child says 'dog bark', you might reply 'Yes, the dog is barking. He wants his dog biscuits.'

These are positive ways of responding to your child's developing language and will encourage him to keep on talking. If we start correcting every mistake, the child will very quickly learn that it is easier not to talk at all.

Between **two and three years** of age, children develop the ability to understand many complex sentences. They can select correct items from a choice of five upon request; they can identify objects by function, for example, 'Which one do we eat with?'; and they can sit and listen to a story for 10 to 20 minutes. They ask lots of *what*, *where* and *who* questions and can sing several nursery rhymes. They can carry on a conversation and be understood most of the time by their family. It is important to note that a child's speech often starts off clear and then deteriorates as they start joining more words together. Although variation is enormous, the guideline is that when he reaches the age of three your child should be intelligible to strangers about 75 per cent of the time. At this stage we would expect children to be saying all the vowel sounds — a, e, i, o, u — clearly and the consonants — p, b, m, n, d, f, w, h, y.

At about the age of three some children will repeat words especially when they are excited or anxious. It can be a worry for a parent if your child comes up to you saying 'I-I-I-I fell over'. Many children go through this stage of dysfluency but only a few of these children go on to become stutterers.

By now your child will be more assertive and confident and this will be reflected in more adult-like body language. He will understand sharing and be more aware of personal space and other people's

TODDLERS WHO ARE SLOWER TO TALK

Although most children are producing recognisable words and simple sentences at about two years of age, some are not. This can cause considerable concern among parents, who see other children of the same age chatting away and it can also be increasingly frustrating for the toddler.

It's worth remembering that first words are related to your child's needs and interests; no child will talk unless there is a need to. If your child is the strong, silent type, it may be that you are looking after him so well that you are anticipating all his needs and he has no need to talk. Try being a little less efficient! Give your child a chance to let you know he is thirsty.

If your child is old enough to look after himself by getting his own drink, it may be necessary to make life more inconvenient so that he needs to ask. When you're dealing with an independent toddler who insists on looking after himself, it may help to have a balance whereby he can get certain drinks on his own but needs to ask you to get others. Have the juice in the door of the fridge so he can help himself but have the milk on the top shelf so he needs to ask for it.

This can be a useful strategy to convey the idea that you want him to talk and that speech is a useful tool for getting what he wants. Children want to convey messages, but they don't mind how they go about it. If pointing and grunting get the desired result, why should he have to say the word?

We are not advocating a stand-up battle of wills. No matter what the age of your child there is no advantage in adding too much pressure and demanding speech. It does not help to refuse to cooperate with your child until he speaks — this can make him feel worried about communicating. If your child is not talking by the time he is two, a speech pathologist will be able to offer specific advice.

feelings, which is in sharp contrast to the earlier world where 'me' dominated all his thoughts and actions. Now, if you're feeling sad, chances are he will be sad too. If he is with a group of children he will now move closer to them to indicate he wants to play with them. Observing and therefore understanding your child's body language goes a long way to creating a positive relationship between the two of you. It is difficult to imagine a life where either oral language or body language is missing. Words explain facts about the world, body language explains emotional states. It is possible to judge the emotional state of a child or adult by observing their breathing rate, their level of eye contact or their stance.

Learning basic concepts

Once your child's language ability begins to grow, he will be able to cope with concepts like positions and colours. Positions can be encouraged throughout the day. Where's your ball? *Under* the table. Put your cup *on* the bench. The water is *in* the bucket. Sources such as books, television and songs, which are all very valuable in teaching these concepts, are covered in detail in Chapters 6 and 7.

When has a word or concept been learnt? Be guided by your child. If he is getting bored and doesn't wish to cooperate, move on. We have met one very distressed parent who was concerned that her three-year-old was no longer able to 'do' a 'tricky' puzzle. On talking to the child it was quite clear that he had done it once and that was enough for him. Providing a variety of puzzles renewed his interest.

What? Why? When? How?
Children constantly ask questions. Although these questions may be wearisome, it is how he learns and how he increases his vocabulary.

GRASPING GRAMMAR

By **three years** of age, the child's memory and forethought have developed so that he is no longer restricted to the 'here and now', but can often remember what happened yesterday and can plan for tomorrow. The three-year-old can talk about many things.

At the same time, he still makes some sound errors. While a large number of sounds are now being used some may still be immature, with one sound substituted for another ('bish' for 'fish'). The three-year-old will rarely leave out sounds except when there are two consonants together, so he may still say 'boon' for 'spoon'. The *k* and *g* sounds are now being used consistently but the *s* sound may still be sounding like a *th* so he sounds like he is lisping.

He is using nouns to name objects, adjectives to describe them and verbs to tell you what they do. He is using '-ed' for the past tense as in 'dropped'. He is starting to slot in the small words between the main ones ('Daddy's car is in the garage'). He has some grasp of grammar ('a ball' and 'two balls'), although he will still make some errors ('Me not want it').

He continues demanding to know *what, why, when* and *how*; and while this can be wearisome, it is how he learns and how he increases his vocabulary and other language skills.

At **four years** of age, a child's sentences are becoming more and more sophisticated, as is his thinking and indeed his play.

He still makes some grammatical errors but some of these are, in fact, 'clever mistakes', which shows that the child has learnt and can use the rules of language. A sentence such as 'I swimmed over there' shows that he understands the rule for past tense: when we talk about something that has happened we put an '-ed' on the end. He has yet to learn that there are in fact exceptions to this rule!

Similarly, 'Look! Two mouses!' shows that he understands the rule for plural nouns: when there is more than one, we put an '-s' on the end. Once again, he has yet to learn that in English there are exceptions to this rule. At a later stage, when he is at school, your child will learn that not all words follow the rules and he will start to use irregular forms such as 'swam' and 'mice' correctly.

Indeed, most children learn grammar — the rules of language — without anyone teaching them. If your child has a significant problem, such as the words being in the incorrect order, or if he still speaks like a text message when he is three, a full assessment will help clarify which areas need to be worked on.

However, if your child makes only occasional and common grammatical and language errors, the suggestions on the following pages should help him to overcome them and at the same time expand his vocabulary. Many of these suggestions make use of the techniques explained on pages 24–25.

By four years your child will be using quite complex sentences and this progression continues right through the next two years. Complex sentences such as 'Dad went to work and we played cricket' and 'I'm going to the library because my friend will be there too' become commonplace. He will use words such as 'would' and 'could' and can tell a familiar story without any pictures or cues. He can follow a series of three directions as well as identify absurdities in a picture. He can tell whether two words rhyme and he can locate the source of sound and distinguish between loud and soft.

FINE-TUNING

As your child hits that magical school age of five, his language is continuing to develop. He understands many more concepts such as 'some', 'many', 'right' and 'left' and he can put five pictures in the right order to sequence a story. During this next year, your child will be able to answer questions such as 'What happens if you don't have an umbrella in the rain?' and 'Why should we wear a coat in winter?' He will be more aware of the significance of time, will use words such as 'yesterday' and 'tomorrow' in his speech, will tell you the opposite of a word and probably his address and telephone number. Aside from the odd error, his grammar virtually matches that of an adult.

HELPING TO CORRECT COMMON MISTAKES

Plurals If your child doesn't use plurals, such as 'two cars', try pairs-memory games, matching to find more than one picture or object while saying 'one car ... two cars!'

'I' and 'me' Some children use 'me' when they mean 'I', as in 'me do it'. This is a difficult one, because if you model the word 'me', the child is confused as to whom you are talking about. The best way is to pick up his hand and pat his chest while modelling the sentence: 'I'll do that.'

Confusing genders Some children don't differentiate between the two genders. Playing with dolls and dressing them up gives you the opportunity to model and practise: 'his pants, his hat, her bag, her chair'. You can also make pictures of objects that are his or hers. Try looking at pictures of people and describing what they are doing: 'he is cooking', 'she is painting'. Exaggerate the words 'he' and 'she', then you can start encouraging him to use the correct words.

Similarly, your child might use the possessive when it's not required, as in 'her jumping over the rope'. Modelling and exaggerating the correct word is also helpful here.

'Doing' Perhaps your child overuses this word, especially in response to a question: 'What's she doing?' 'She doing over a rope.' The first step is to encourage use of the action word, in this case 'jumping'. Your child might then progress to saying 'She doing jumping over a rope.' Explain that he didn't have to say 'doing'. You can make a game of throwing the 'doing' into the rubbish bin. Point out also that you need the small word 'is': 'She is jumping over a rope.' A hand signal can help remind your child to use 'is'. Point out that it is such a little word and use your thumb and forefinger to indicate this. Use this signal each time you model the word.

Colours Colours are often a sticking point for children. Try associating the colour with something in the environment and use this reference each time you name the colour: 'Your jumper is blue like the sky.' Others are 'yellow like the sun', 'green like the grass' and 'red like blood' (children always remember this one!).

Size Contrasting sizes helps make the point to your children. Try not to restrict your child's use of concepts by always describing things as 'big' or 'little' — try using 'fat' or 'thin', 'long' or 'short', 'wide' or 'narrow'.

Prepositions When modelling prepositions — in, on, under, beside, behind, in front of — work on only two at a time. For example, hide toys around the room: *in* the box, *under* the table, *in* the doll's house, *under* the chair.

Same and different Picture pairs is a very useful game to point out when pictures are the same and when they are different. Some children have trouble with the concept of being different until it is shown as being 'not the same'.

Describing words Try to expose your child to a variety of words. Rather than making yours too simple, remember to keep your language above your child's own skill level. For example, if you describe your friend as 'good', how will your child learn about 'funny', 'kind', 'happy', 'lively', 'cheerful' or 'helpful'?

Grouping words Extend the range and grouping of words by asking your child to think of all the things he can wear, all the things he can ride on or in, or all the things he can eat. Maybe cut out pictures and make posters of different word groups.

Sequencing Draw a sequence of actions on different pieces of paper. For example, draw a child with nothing on, with his underwear on, with his underwear and jumper on, with his jumper and trousers on, and with his jumper, trousers and shoes on; then ask your child to place them in the right order.

Talking, Listening, Encouraging, Finding Time
Listen carefully to his stories, as indeed you would
like him to listen to yours.

By **five years** of age, your child will be talking almost as well as you. Certainly, his vocabulary will expand throughout his life, but he now knows most of the rules of his language and can use it appropriately. Communicating with your child can be a most rewarding experience. As your child becomes increasingly independent, the only way of discovering his interests and ideas, sharing opinions with him or even discussing what he has been up to, is to communicate.

There is still some finetuning that needs to occur. Speech sounds sharpen up and the last of the sounds, notably *r* and *th*, will develop. The use of irregular verbs will expand and the errors become less frequent. At long last 'I falled over' becomes 'I fell over.'

Once a child is speaking fluently there is a tendency to assume that all speech and language skills have been acquired. This is not true as our language continues to develop in many other ways. It's a bit like learning to drive. It doesn't take long to learn how to move the car backwards and forwards and even turn corners, but there is a lot of experience and knowledge about other road users that still needs to be gained. It is the same with speech and language skills: once your child has acquired clear speech with a wide and varied vocabulary and can construct grammatically complex sentences, he has to continue learning how to use these skills to form friendships as well as to progress academically.

The importance of the use of language is particularly evident in children who have a language disorder, Asperger's syndrome or semantic pragmatic disorder. These children may eventually develop clear fluent speech but still miss many of the cues in their environment so they stand out and appear different. The symptoms and implications of these and other speech and language disorders are covered in Chapter 4.

At a milder level we have all met people who don't seem to listen or don't look at you when they are speaking. Or other people who encroach on our personal space. These are all very important aspects of communication.

So once your child is talking fluently, stimulation shouldn't end. There is no substitute for time and conversation. Not only will his language structures be extended but he will develop the ways in which he *uses* his language — his pragmatic skills.

Most of the techniques we have discussed in the previous sections are still relevant for the school-age child. They are summarised here as a reminder.

- Continue talking to your child about what things are, where you find them and how they work.
- Take your discussions a stage further by working out alternatives and different possible outcomes: 'What do you think is inside?' 'What do you think might happen next?'
- Encourage him to express his views and feelings: 'Do you think he liked that?' 'What was your favourite part?' 'Why did you like that?'
- Once your child can read by himself, don't abandon those quiet times reading together. Try reading children's novels. There is a great variety available, and you can always seek advice from your local librarian.
- Practise what you preach: if your child sees you reading, he will be more inclined to enjoy books himself.
- Encourage your child to ask questions.
- Take the time to play with your child and enjoy his company.
- Listen carefully to his stories, as indeed you would like him to listen to yours.
- Find time to talk about your day. Make sure everyone has a turn. Be realistic — not every day is a good one but talking is an emotional outlet for everyone to discuss difficulties and find ways of solving them.
- Reduce background noise during family conversation time.
- Monitor television viewing (see Chapter 6). Talk together about what you have seen.

Your child is probably at school by now, but there are three areas of language that can still be readily extended within the home. These are vocabulary, concepts and pragmatic skills.

Vocabulary

This is probably the easiest aspect of language to develop and where progress is most obvious. It is always a surprise when children start using words they have learnt somewhere else, especially words that their parents don't use!

Vocabulary continues developing throughout our lives. Through our reading and conversations we are always learning new vocabulary. Some words we understand but might not use for a variety of reasons: it might not be culturally appropriate, not our style or too formal for everyday use. Your child will also discover that a whole range of words can mean similar but not exactly the same thing. The words 'big', 'large', 'fat', 'huge', 'enormous', 'gigantic', although similar, conjure up different images in our minds. Your support can help extend this vocabulary and along with it your child's general knowledge.

Remember, when we learn new words, understanding precedes expression. Occasionally we hear people use a word inappropriately and that is usually because they have misunderstood what the word means. Words used inappropriately can especially irritate older people. While most of vocabulary expansion is just a learning process, as parents we also need to keep in touch with the 'cool' words. These are words that may have been picked up from television programs or at school and often mean something different from what they meant when we were growing up. We can still remember when one of our children first came home from school calling everything 'wicked'. After a dozen attempts to explain the original meaning of the word we gave up and started to accept the importance of the peer group and also the flexible nature of language.

If a person has a wide vocabulary of words he understands but is not using these words in conversation, then he may have a problem with *word retrieval*. The difference between receptive vocabulary and word retrieval can be demonstrated in the following way. If you place a range of pictures in front of your child and ask him to find you one of them, this is checking his comprehension of words. However, if you place pictures one at a time on the table and ask him to name them, this is checking his ability to retrieve words from his vocabulary store. Word-finding difficulties can show up in speech in different ways:

- Lots of pauses.
- Use of filler words while trying to think, for example, 'um'.
- Non-specific words such as 'thing' or 'stuff' are over used. 'Can you put the thing on the thing?'
- Descriptions are used instead of the word:
  Q What would you like to drink?
  A The one with the green lid.
- Use of totally different words that start with the same sound as the target word, for example, 'swimming pool' might become 'swapping pool'.
- Use of words with similar, but not exactly, the same meaning, for example, 'pot' instead of 'cup'.

In the last two examples the child may vary the substituted word every time he uses it and may sometimes use it correctly.

Difficulties retrieving frequently used words can be a sign of more complex language or learning difficulties.

Vocabulary is much more likely to expand if it relates to areas of interest. So if little Johnny has a passion for dinosaurs then reading about, playing or discussing dinosaurs is going to improve not only his vocabulary and general knowledge but will also teach him new words and concepts about the earth, parts of the body and what they are used for, time and survival. This is much more beneficial than trying to force an interest where there isn't one. It is worth keeping a developmental level in mind, but in our opinion, it is easier to simplify a complex issue than force an interest where there isn't one.

Everyday activities offer plenty of opportunities for new vocabulary. A trip to the doctor can offer a wealth of words such as 'stethoscope', 'thermometer', 'measure' and 'temperature'.

Expanding vocabulary related to feelings gives your child a chance to learn about body language and expressions; and to expand his understanding of and ability to respond to observations of others. Given the right words your child will also learn how to understand and express his own emotions through the use of words rather than physically. If your child can express his feelings it makes it easier for you as a parent to deal effectively with the problem; consoling a crying child when you have no idea of the cause can be frustrating.

When you are reading to your child occasionally check on difficult words and see if your child knows what they mean or perhaps you can work it out together. In this way he will start developing the skill of working out word meanings from the context or other clues available. If you also don't know a word — and some words in dinosaur books can be tricky — admit that you don't know it and look it up in the dictionary together. By doing this, your child will realise it is all right to admit he doesn't know, and he will learn a way of finding out the meaning of words.

If your child is multilingual then he might discover that some words don't translate easily or that some words or phrases are culturally biased. This is all part of discovering different aspects of language.

Concepts

As your child gets older he will be exposed to a wider range of concepts, many of them specifically taught within the classroom, particularly through mathematics.

Same/different This is such a useful concept as it enables us to talk and describe many other objects, people and activities. Matching-pairs games are a great way to start learning this concept. Point out what the differences are in the pictures.

Number sense This is not only when we can sequence numbers by rote but also when counting corresponds to the number of items. At first when asked to count, some children will just set off by rote, often exceeding the number of items. It helps to physically move the objects and count slowly, matching speech to movement.

Time (yesterday, tomorrow, now, later, year, month, morning, afternoon etc.) At first young children have no concept of time past or time to wait. If your child has a special party in the afternoon he will probably keep asking 'Is it time yet?' even though you have told him it will not be until later that day.

To aid the understanding of days you could keep a weekly calendar so that he learns routines according to the day. For example: on Mondays you go shopping, Tuesdays you go to Kindergym etc.

The telling of time by the clock can be difficult for many children until upper-junior primary. You can help make the concept more concrete by referring to an activity that starts on the hour and pointing to the hands on the clock at that time. If his favourite television program starts at 4 p.m. get him to watch the clock and see when the small hand is on the four with the big hand pointing straight up.

Order (next, last, first, second etc.) Lining up at school, taking turns in games, having or watching races and even making patterns all help develop the understanding of order.

Position (between, next to, behind, left, right etc.) Start with easy positions such as 'in' and 'on' then add further contrasting positions such as 'in front'.

Quantity (lots, least, more than, most etc.) Children can be very quick to work out someone has *more* than they do. But they may need some help expanding their range of vocabulary covering these concepts.

Measurement (size, distance, volume.) These concepts, like most of the others, develop through your child exploring the environment around him. This is where sand and water play really come into their own. Filling containers and building towers prompts questions such as 'Will all the sand from this jug go into the bucket?'

Comparatives (big, bigger, biggest; colder, hotter etc.) If your child is stuck on these it is easier to play games to demonstrate your point. The problem with comparatives is it depends on the given items before a decision can be made. Change one of the items and the answer may

BASIC LANGUAGE CONCEPTS

Size

big	wide	thin	thick
tall	large	narrow	small
short	long	fat	

comparatives based on sizes given above e.g. biggest / smallest

Position / direction

in	top	low	far
on	in front	middle	underneath
behind	over	bottom	outside / inside
beside	below	corner	right way up
under	around	high	upside-down
up	above	centre	forward / backwards
down	along	side	
before	through	close to	
after	between	straight	
next		edge	
		highest	
		near	

Quality

first	as many as	whole
second	most	lot / lots of
last	half	least
in a row	few	some

Volume / weight

less	more
as much as	heavy
full	light
empty	

Other

every	pair
same	order
different	matching
alike	except
	none

change. If you are playing with toy cars, find the biggest of them all. Add another car: is it *still* the biggest?

Many concepts are abstract in nature. It is easier to understand concrete concepts that are here and now and that you can see and manipulate but it is harder to understand concepts not in front of you. Therefore your child will understand 'big' and 'small' before he grasps that an object can be big but there is another even 'bigger'.

Pragmatic Skills

We discussed in earlier chapters how before your child can even speak, he is working out the rules of conversation and learning to understand subtle clues associated with language. A child works out extremely early that the tone of voice and varying body language can alter the meaning of what is said. Someone not looking at you as you speak may be bored so you might change your conversation or move away because you think they are not interested. These pragmatic skills of how we use our language continue developing through childhood. They are most important for developing social skills and forming relationships. Children discover that there are many different ways of using their language. They discover the language and manner they use to speak to their peers may not be acceptable to Granny. They may learn to soften a request so they are more likely to get what they want. Most of us have experiences of other parents commenting on our children's good behaviour and manners, while we are wondering why they don't behave and speak like that at home. The child has learnt what is expected of them and can apply these when necessary, but in a safe environment at home he is still using language to discover limits and boundaries.

As your child gets older he will be able to discuss topics for longer and longer periods, sharing information as well as asking questions. He will also learn the art of storytelling — what information to give or omit or even to embellish the story to get the response he requires from different people. Their stories will start to have a beginning, middle and an end or a consequence. There will be a plot and key figures in a story.

With the increase in vocabulary and as your child begins to understand the nuances of language he will begin to understand

BASIC CHECKLIST OF PRAGMATIC SKILLS

- Does your child use eye contact appropriately?

- Can he take turns during a conversation?

- Can he understand the use of tone and intonation in the speaker?

- Can he use appropriate and varying tones and intonation when speaking?

- Can he use language to greet people?

- Can he initiate and terminate a conversation appropriately?

- Can he sequence information correctly?

- Can he listen to the speaker?

- Can he ask and answer questions?

- Can he ask for information?

- Can he use language to make choices?

- If his peers don't like his behaviour can he work out what it is that he has said or done that is unacceptable?

- Can he change his behaviour to be accepted by his peers if he wants to be?

- Can he predict the outcome of what might happen?

- Is he able to give an opinion and express his feelings?

- Is he able to ask questions to help him sort out the nature of the problem?

- Can he learn from past experiences and make comparisons?

- Can he group and define ideas?

- Can he explain his view to prove a point?

- Can he give reasons for his behaviour? Respond to 'Why did you do that?'

sarcasm, phrases and sayings. When you say 'pigs might fly' your child realises that you don't mean this literally and it is implausible. Children also need to use language to think of the implications of what you asked without you having to say everything.

The way we use our language to communicate is so very important and although a problem in this area may have been evident for some time, it is often when a child goes to school and is seen alongside other children the problem becomes more obvious. Children with significant problems in this area may have a semantic pragmatic disorder or a problem along the autism spectrum. They may be insensitive to the needs of others, and don't pick up clues from the conversation, gestures or body language. These children may continue to interpret language literally in a concrete way and miss the subtleties of language such as the meaning of the expression: 'Pull your socks up.' They are often not able to stay on the same topic of conversation and may change it without warning or return to a recurring topic they are interested in.

Pragmatic skills are not only important for social development but also for the progression of academic abilities. Language is necessary to solve problems and work out consequences and implications.

Here is a summary of the important ways in which we use our pragmatic skills.

- *Getting on with other people.* To do this we need to know how to greet them appropriately, and ask polite questions (whether or not we are interested).
- *Making things happen.* As adults we know there are different ways we can try and make things happen in our environment. We can cooperate with others or make suggestions and try and persuade someone to our way of thinking. We could be much firmer and instruct people or order them to carry out a task. If we are desperate we may even threaten to get what we want.
- *Working out what will happen in the future.* Here we really make our language skills work hard. At times we make guesses about what may happen or we may make a prediction using the information we already have. We may need to calculate what may be the outcome given previous consequences in similar situations.

If we have our own goal we would like to achieve we may have to design the steps we need to take to achieve that goal.

- *Expressing ourselves.* We express ourselves daily as we tell stories or provide information. We give away a lot of information about our own personalities as we express our opinions and feelings.
- *Problem solving.* When making a decision we set out all sides of any problem and we may need to ask questions to gather the information required. We might need to compare ideas, group and define our thoughts to help us formulate a solution.

3 Learning to speak clearly

Speech, or articulation, refers to the sounds that come out of our mouth and how these sounds form words. The speech process involves a coordinated pattern of movements by our tongue, lips, teeth and palate.

Like language development, articulation development follows an orderly sequence and is acquired over the first seven years. Vowel sounds are acquired before consonant sounds and are less likely to be misarticulated. Please note that we are talking about *sounds* not letters. The actual sounds we use vary from language to language. Your baby will shape up the sounds that are appropriate to the language he is learning.

In the **first three months** of life, a baby's coos are a signal he is learning to say vowel sounds such as the long 'ahhhhhh'. After this comes the babbling stage where the infant joins a consonant and vowel sound together, such as 'ba-ba-ba', 'wa-wa-wa' and 'ma-ma-ma'.

Initially it will be sounds that are relatively easy to produce. He will start with one syllable and then progress to two. In the **first three years** of life probably only those closest to your child will understand everything he says; you may have to interpret for others. At first he may omit sounds at the end of words and even substitute easy sounds for the harder ones. Consonant blends, where there are two or more consonants together, are frequently reduced to one sound, for example he will say 'bu' instead of 'blue' or 'wing' instead of 'swing'. As the toddler says more and more individual words, his speech will become more and more intelligible as he has more practice producing the different speech sounds. The exception to this, for children with 'normally' developing speech, is they sometimes lose clarity as they start to say long sentences simply because they are trying to say so many new unpractised words. This corrects itself with maturity. The other exception, of course, is if your child has a specific speech problem. However, research has shown that by three years of age children can be understood by strangers 75 per cent of the time.

Consonants are grouped according to how the sound is made, where in the mouth it is made and whether or not they use voice. Often in therapy, sounds are taught as a group rather than individually. Without becoming too technical it is worth understanding how the earlier sounds can be grouped together. It may be useful to refer to the Oral Muscles diagram on the opposite page.

Nasal sounds
- *m*, *n* and *ng*: a block is made somewhere in the mouth and air channelled through the nose. For example, the lips close for *m*.

Stop consonants
- *p* and *b* are made with the lips;
- *t* and *d* are made with the tongue tip against the alveolar ridge;
- *k* and *g* are made with the back of the tongue against the soft palate.

The sounds *p*, *t* and *k* are produced on a whisper and are therefore voiceless. The sounds *b*, *d* and *g* are loud sounds and are made with a strong voice.

Long sounds

- *f* and *v* are made with the top teeth and bottom lip;
- *s* and *z* are made with the tongue tip behind the top teeth;
- *sh* is made by pushing the lips open.

The sounds are made when the air is blown through a narrow opening. Once again, the sounds *f*, *s* and *sh* are quiet or voiceless.

All other sounds are more complex and guidance should be sought from a speech pathologist.

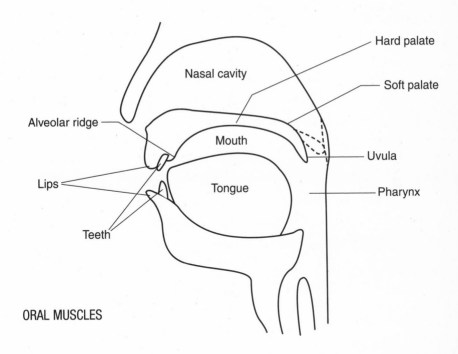

ORAL MUSCLES

From **three years** of age, sounds develop rapidly until five when all except for *r*, *v* and *th* are used correctly. The Sound Chart on page 46 provides an easy reference about the ages at which sounds develop.

SOUND CHART
Which consonant sounds develop when?

SOUND	AGES						
	3	3½	4	4½	5	6	7
p	✖						
b	✖						
m	✖						
h	✖						
w	✖						
n	✖						
t	✖						
d	✖						
g	✖						
ng	✖						
y	✖						
k		✖					
f		✖					
l			✖				
sh			✖				
ch			✖				
s				✖			
z				✖			
j				✖			
r					✖		
v						✖	
th							✖

Around 75 per cent of all children are correctly producing these sounds at the above ages. Consonant blends (where two consonants occur together) such as 'swing', 'spoon' and 'blue' are mastered between four and six years of age.
Source: Kilminster & Laird, *Australian Journal of Human Communication Disorders*, 1983

The consonant-blend sounds are becoming clearer by five. These include *fr*, *gl*, *cr* and *br*. Often those blends involving the *s* and *th* sounds develop even later. Words such as 'slippery dip' and 'throw' are tricky, even for six-year-olds! The sounds most likely to cause problems for children when they start school are *s* and *r*, remembering that five-year-olds are not expected to say the *th* sound accurately until they are seven.

Specific problems with sounds can be identified well before three. We see children for therapy who present as bright with good understanding, but who have difficulty producing sounds. One cute little two-year-old comes in each week, tugs on his therapist's sleeve and cheerfully says 'a oh'. Mum quickly follows on by saying 'hello'. He does not use any consonant sounds at all. If you are concerned with your child's use of speech sounds, a speech pathologist will be able to give specific advice, but again, there is much you can do yourself and 'sound play' can be great fun. The Mr Tongue game (see page 49) is a fun way to practise oral movements which are necessary for clear speech development. The game should be played in front of a mirror large enough to see two faces.

How else can we have fun with sounds? For some entertaining ways to teach your child how to make different sounds refer to pages 50–51 on How Do We Make Speech Sounds? There are also plenty of games you can play with your child to teach him about sounds, using objects or pictures which start with the target sound. Some of these sound games are given on page 52. Remember, before your child can say a sound in a word, he needs to be able to say it on its own.

Encouraging clear speech

Studies have shown that parents respond differently according to whether their young child has well-developed or slowly developing speech. The more an infant vocalises, the greater the frequency of response from the parent. In turn, this results in increased social interaction and imitation of more speech. Hence the positive cycle continues.

Given what you now know about the development of speech sounds, remember to expect errors. You will not improve your child's speech by forcing him to say the *v* sound correctly when he is only three!

Be a good listener and make sure your child knows you are listening to him. Use positive body language to show your interest in what he is saying. Do not correct every sound error he makes or you run the risk of discouraging him from talking. The less he talks, the less chance he has of improving his speech clarity.

The single most important thing you can do to help your child learn to speak clearly is to be a good speech model yourself. Children learn by listening and copying, therefore you need to speak slowly and clearly if you wish them to do the same. Most children learn to repeat your correct model and self-correct spontaneously; they will learn to speak more clearly this way than if they are forced to repeat everything they don't say perfectly.

An issue, which causes us concern at times, is when parents pretend they have understood what their child says. They might say 'Yes dear, that's right' and not have a clue what their child said. If you think your child doesn't know when you haven't understood him, you're wrong! We have had two-year-olds who are sufficiently aware of their inability to talk clearly that they know when you haven't understood them. This tends to leave them frustrated and upset; they must feel let down. It is better to say to your child 'Mummy didn't quite understand what you were saying. Can you tell me again?' or, if appropriate, 'Show me what you were talking about?' If you understood some of their words do let them know as this will provide positive reinforcement.

Whenever we pretend to understand their speech, we are not increasing expectations on them to speak more clearly. Why bother? Mum understands everything I say. Not true! In a non-threatening way, it is possible to discuss with your child the need for him to be clearer when speaking. Say something like:

> *'We know you can talk really well but sometimes you go a bit too fast. We'd like you to slow down because you have lots of great things to say and people love talking with you. Now let's just say that again slowly and clearly.'*

Use whatever words seem appropriate for the age and intellectual capacity of your child. There is no need to stop him every time he speaks, but just often enough to remind him. If your child is receiving therapy for a speech problem then your speech pathologist will advise on how often to remind and ask him to 'Say it again.'

As well as the fun activities listed in the Sound Games, there are some other specific ways you can encourage clearer speech as your child is developing. It is common for some preschool-aged children to speak too quickly. This results in poor clarity and sometimes 'mumbly'

MR TONGUE

One day Mr Tongue opened his front door and came outside (poke out tongue). He looked at his house and saw it was very dirty. Mr Tongue decided to clean his house.

'What will I clean first?' he said. 'Look how dirty the windows are — I'll clean them.'

So he cleaned the top windows on the inside and outside (*lick front and back of top teeth*), and the bottom windows (*lick front and back of bottom teeth*). Then he cleaned the door (*lick along bottom and across top lip carefully*).

Next, Mr Tongue decided to clean the:

- steps   *lick down to chin*

- floor   *lick bottom of mouth*

- ceiling   *lick back along roof of mouth*

- walls   *poke tongue from side to side pushing out cheeks*

- chimney   *blow through lips making them vibrate*

When he had finished cleaning his house, Mr Tongue nailed the pictures up in the back of his house K-K-K-K-K, and in the front of his house t-t-t-t.

Mr Tongue came outside and looked at his lovely clean house (*poke out tongue*) and was very pleased. After doing all that work he felt very tired so he went back inside, closed the door and went to sleep (*pull in tongue and close lips*).

HOW DO WE MAKE SPEECH SOUNDS?

You can help your child learn how to make sounds not only by saying them but also by explaining what we do when we say them. Children learn more easily if we can use something to represent the sound. Exaggerate the sound when you say it. It may help him to watch your face as you make the sound.

Select a sound your child is able to copy and stick to that one for a short period of time. At this stage we are concerned with sounds only, so don't worry about the way words are spelt. For example, the sound *k* is the initial sound in 'car', 'cat' and 'key', and the sound *s* is the initial sound in 'sand', 'circus' and 'celery'.

Here is a list of sounds and the way we make them.

m   The car says 'mmm'. Put your lips together and hum. Feel the vibrations on the side of your nose.

p   Make the candle flicker by saying 'p-p-p'. Put your lips together then quickly open them feeling the air on your hand.

b   The bouncing ball says 'b-b-b'. Put your lips together and then open them with a loud sound.

n   The jackhammer says 'nnn'. Put the tip of your tongue behind your top teeth and say 'no'. Feel the vibrations on the side of your nose.

w   The crying baby says 'w-w-w'. Put your lips forward as if you're about to whistle.

t   The dripping tap says 't-t-t'. Put the tip of your tongue up behind your top teeth and then let it drop down.

h   When the puppy dog pants he says 'h-h-h'. Open your mouth and puff on the back of your hand.

d   When we bang the drum we say 'd-d-d'. Put the tip of your tongue up behind your top teeth and make a loud sound as you drop your tongue down.

k   The shooting gun says 'k-k-k'. Open your mouth and pretend you're going to cough. Put your finger on your tongue to push it down and the back of the tongue will jump up to make the sound. If your child still finds this sound hard to produce, get him to practise gargling. This encourages the tongue into the right position.

g   The water going down the plughole says 'g-g-g'. Do the same as for *k* but make a loud noise.

y   The yoyo says 'y-y-y'. Spread your lips out in a smile and put the tip of your tongue down behind your bottom teeth.

l   When we sing we say 'la-la-la'. Put the tip of your tongue up behind your top teeth and then drop it down. Do not use your lips.

f   The rabbit says 'fff' with his big front teeth. Bite your bottom lip with your top teeth and blow.

v   The aeroplane engine says 'vvv'. Do the same as for *f* but make it a loud noise.

s   The snake says 'sss'. Put your teeth together, spread your lips in a smile and put the tip of your tongue up behind your top teeth.

z   The buzzing bee says 'zzz'. Do the same as for *s* but make a loud noise.

ch   The train says 'ch-ch-ch'. Put your teeth together, the tip of your tongue up behind your top teeth and make a quiet explosion.

j   Put your teeth together, the tip of your tongue up behind your top teeth and make a loud explosion.

sh   When we want someone to be quiet we say 'sh-sh'. Push your lips forward and do the same as for *s*.

r   The roaring lion says 'rrr'. Curl your tongue up in your mouth and smile.

th   Poke your tongue out between your teeth and blow.

SOUND GAMES

Bingo Use two playing boards of pictures (one each) and collect matching small pictures of objects starting with the chosen sound. Each player places his playing board in front of him on the table. Place the small cards face down in a pile in the middle. The first player takes a card from the top of the pile and says the name of the picture on the card. He then places this card on the matching picture on his or your playing board. Players continue in turn. The first player to cover all the pictures on his board calls out 'Bingo!' and is the winner.

Lucky dip Place objects in a pillowcase or box. Your child can pick out one at a time and together you can practise naming it.

Fishing Collect together pictures of objects with the chosen sound. Make a fishing rod with a stick, a piece of string and a magnet. Put paperclips on each picture and place the pictures in a box or bowl. Your child can name the pictures as he catches them.

Picture pairs Cut out two pictures of objects starting with each of the chosen sounds. Place them face down on the table. Take it in turns to turn over two pictures, naming each one, until you find the matching pair.

Cutting and pasting Make a special sound scrapbook.

Hide and seek Hide objects around a room, and your child can name each one as he finds them.

Skittles Stand the objects up like skittles. Roll a ball and name each object as you hit it.

What's missing? Use objects or pictures and spread three or more face up in a row on a table in front of the child. The child says the name of the pictures in order from left to right. Then ask the child to close his eyes while you take one away. He has to name the missing one. If he does not guess it straight away, you might give him a clue.

speech. Choose some longer words and have your child listen to you tap out each syllable (or part) of the word. Take his hand and tap out each syllable slowly as you say the word again. Either tap his hand on the table or on his leg as clapping the syllables is more noisy and therefore distracting. He needs to be able to hear the sounds in the word. This is a very effective technique for slowing down your child's speech. It also makes him more aware of the individual sounds in the word and helps him to say the more 'tricky' words of our language.

Start off demonstrating with two-syllable words such as 'ha-mmer' and 'le-tter' then move on to three-syllable words such as 'bu-tter-fly', 'am-bu-lance' and 'di-no-saur'. Later come the four-syllable words such as 'he-li-cop-ter' and 'ste-go-sau-rus'. Hopefully by this stage your child will only need a reminder when he tries to say one of these words for the first time. It is easy to make this a fun activity by choosing words your child is interested in. If he is keen on dinosaurs then it's easy as there are plenty of long words within that subject! Link this practice with a theme that the preschool or class teacher is using and this will make it more meaningful for your child. If they are going on a trip to the vet or to the hospital, collect pictures of relevant words and play hide-and-seek with the pictures, saying each word as you find them. Even seven-year-olds enjoy this activity.

Children from preschool age onwards like to make a 'Good Talking' chart which can hang on the fridge or in some other prominent place as a reminder. Talk to your child about how to be a clear speaker. It might go along the lines of:

My Good Talking Chart
1 Stand near the person you are talking to.
2 Use your eyes to look at the other person's eyes.
3 Speak slowly.
4 Speak quietly (implying you don't 'yell')
or use a nice voice.
5 Now I'm a good clear talker!

Let them decorate the chart with stickers and/or draw pictures to illustrate each point.

Often we try to change a pattern in our child's speech when he is not even aware of the behaviour himself. This relates particularly to children who speak too quickly or too loudly most of the time. You can say 'Slow down' or 'Talk quietly' until you're worn out and the child won't change at all because he doesn't know in what way he is being too fast or too noisy. You can increase his awareness by recording each other on a cassette-player. This will provide immediate feedback as to how you are speaking and how he is speaking. Choose activities where your child doesn't need to think of the words, such as rote-learned tasks like saying the alphabet or a nursery rhyme or re-telling a short story. Firstly, you say it very quickly and then replay it and ask for his opinion.

'Could you understand everything Mum said? Was it easy to listen to?'

Hopefully, he will say 'No'. Now say the same thing at a slower speed.

'Could you understand Mum this time? Was it easier to listen to?'

Hopefully, he will say 'Yes'. Now it's his turn to try fast and slow talking. If your child is older, ask him to read a short poem. When he is speaking appropriately tell him so he knows what you expect from him:

'Good talking, that's not too fast nor too slow. It's just right.'

Children who are just starting to use a particular speech sound some of the time (indicating they are developmentally ready to do so) can benefit if you pay a little more attention to that sound in incidental ways. When you are talking, stress the sound so your child will become more aware of the correct way to say it, or exaggerate the sound when you hear him say it by simply modelling it back to him.

We discussed the technique of modelling in Chapter 2. For example, if your child says 'I like putting the saddle on the hort' you can just say back to him 'horsssssse' so he can listen to the exaggerated *s* sound. We are not for a moment suggesting you ask your child to copy you every time he says it wrongly, instead you are asking him to listen more closely to the sound.

Once your child can read, books, even simple ones, can be a great way of reinforcing correct sound production. This is particularly the case for the later developing sounds such as *s* and *th*. What better way for your child to listen to, and try to say, the *th* sound as in 'the', 'them' and 'this', than to read the words himself?

Another fun way to increase your child's awareness of speech sounds is for you to say a word incorrectly and see if your child can catch you out. If he can pick your mistake and tell you what it should be, give him lots of praise. If he didn't hear the mistake don't criticise him but rather just say something like 'O-oh, I said "car" wrongly. I said "tar" instead of "car". We don't drive in a "tar" do we?' If he can copy the word correctly praise him, but if he can't, do not correct him. The objective of the game is to have him hear the sounds, not say them.

Identifying a speech problem

A child with a speech problem may do one or more of the following. He may:

- show frustration with the way he speaks or his inability to speak, especially after the age of two;
- not be able to make himself understood by anyone;
- need a parent to interpret for him well beyond the age you would expect it;
- continue to leave off beginnings and ends of words;
- omit entire syllables from words;
- distort his vowel sounds;
- have very unusual sounding speech;
- have some problem with the muscles used for eating or feeding — he may be a particularly messy eater, or have had early difficulties with swallowing and sucking.

The following chapter on speech and language impairment discusses these symptoms in more detail.

PROBLEM SOUND CHART — *th* SOUND

Take your time and don't rush through a step unless you are convinced it has been achieved.

Listen for the sound For your child to use the sound appropriately he needs to be able to hear it and identify it. Practise listening to a range of sounds and identifying when he hears the *th*. At first he may need to be encouraged to watch your mouth for clues. Try listening for the *th* at the beginning or end of words. When you are sure he is aware of the sound move on to the next stage.

Producing the sound Sit with your child in front of a mirror and watch how the sound is made. Ask him to protrude his tongue so that it can just be seen and then blow gently. Practise saying the *th* and *f* sounds until he is aware of the difference.

Producing the sound in syllables By the time you are working on this sound your child should have some knowledge of reading. Write down vowel sounds on a piece of paper. Practise saying the *th* followed by the vowel sound, for example 'th-ee'.

Producing the sound in words beginning with *th* Begin by practising repeating words. Make up pictures of each word or write them down on a piece of paper and play games as previously suggested, for example, bingo, pairs etc, or use the pictures with any board game — you have to name the picture correctly before you have a turn. Only attempt the word two or three times and praise any effort, otherwise you will increase his frustration. When words can be said easily move on to the next stage.

Producing the *th*-practised words in phrases Initially your child may just imitate short phrases but then you may play games as further practice. Once you are confident that words beginning with *th* can be said correctly in simple sentences or phrases repeat the above steps for words ending in *th*. Once that has been achieved commence on words with a *th* in the middle.

Using the sound in conversation If your child is able to produce *th* words in a controlled setting for short periods it is time to encourage their use in conversational speech. You may wish to start with poems or rhymes or practise reading when he can see the *th* word coming. Then encourage him to use the sound in general conversation. At first, expect just a few words to be said correctly; gradually the number will expand. If he does make an error just model the correct pronunciation; your child now knows how to fix it.

For many children a mild speech problem has no direct effect on their development. It is usually the parent who finds it the most irritating. If your child has a lisp or just mispronounces one or two sounds, the chances are he has become used to the way he speaks and doesn't even notice it. Mild speech problems are easy to ignore and his friends have probably not even mentioned it.

If it is just one sound and you know your child is well beyond the age you would expect him to develop it, you may like to try the format described in the Problem Sound Chart above. We have chosen the *th* sound for our example as this is typically substituted and is fairly easy to work on at home.

If the problem is more complex do seek advice. Unless you have received direct advice from a speech pathologist don't make your child repeat mispronounced words. Rather than helping you can cause frustration and disappointment. It is easy to say, but try and be patient. The aim is to keep communication positive.

4 Dealing with speech and language problems

While every child is an individual and develops at his own pace, there are guidelines for what is 'normal' at each age. Your child can be compared to these norms to determine if there are any delays in his development. These guidelines, often referred to as 'developmental milestones' are listed in Chapter 10. Most parents we meet are very astute and seem to know when something is wrong with their child's speech, language or listening skills. However, sometimes it is difficult for them to put their finger on the exact problem. We always tell parents to follow their gut feeling and seek help if they are concerned. We have never known a parent to be wrong yet! You just seem to know when something is 'not quite right'. It is always worth seeking an assessment from a speech pathologist, if only to alleviate your concerns. Some 'problems' are a very normal stage of development and professional reassurance may put your mind at ease.

When a child is being assessed, the speech pathologist will want to determine whether the problem is a developmental delay or a speech or language disorder. A developmental delay means that the child's speech and language are following the normal pathways of development but at a slower rate. This implies the child should eventually catch up, unless there is an intellectual delay as well. In contrast, a speech or language disorder is characterised by unusual and atypical features. A child with a disorder retains these features as he matures and therefore does not grow out of it.

SPEECH DELAY AND DISORDERS
Speech delay

A child with a speech (or articulation) delay typically presents with errors of his sounds, such as omissions (he leaves out a sound and might say 'ba' for 'bat') and substitutions (he uses one sound for another sound such as 'tar' for 'car'). The impact of this delay on the child's speech really depends on the number of sound errors. If he's only misarticulating one or two sounds then this is less of a problem, unless he is much older and should be saying that sound by his age. For example, it is acceptable for a four-year-old to substitute the sound *f* for *th* and therapy would not be recommended. However, if the child is eight and still making this error and perhaps spelling words incorrectly as a consequence (spells 'thing' as 'fing') then intervention would be appropriate. Often it is just one or two sounds that are a problem, typically *s, r, l* or *th*, in which case you could try the following format:

- Learn how to produce the sound on its own in isolation, such as *d*.
- Say the sound *d* joined with a vowel in a nonsense word such as 'dee' or 'da'.
- Practise single real words like 'door' or 'dog'. Your child must be able to say many words beginning with the *d* sound before moving on to the next step.
- Practise the words in short phrases such as 'door open', 'door shut' and 'dog runs'.

- When phrases are clear move on to saying the words in sentences, for example, 'The dog jumped over the fence'.
- Finally, your child starts to use the sound automatically in conversation. This format is used in the Problem Sound Chart for *th* on pages 56–57 in Chapter 3, so you should be able to adapt it for any sound. Keep the practice as fun and positive as possible.

If the child's general speech clarity is affected by a few misarticulations, then a professional opinion may be worthwhile. Once again, if people only misunderstand him once in a while then chances are there is no problem. However if *you* have trouble understanding what he says, then less familiar listeners will have even more trouble and intervention may be necessary. If at any time your child is frustrated by his speech and/or he is self-conscious when talking and lacks confidence, then seeking advice is important. Children who are not confident talkers are more likely to suffer in their social relationships once they start preschool.

If your child is diagnosed with a speech problem, therapy may or may not be recommended. In the case of some delayed-speech problems, your speech pathologist may advise you to spend a couple of months practising specific tasks at home. This may include activities such as those we discussed in Chapter 3. If this is the initial course of action suggested, it does not mean you are being fobbed off or your child is too young. Sometimes it is important to try specific tasks in a natural speaking environment first. If you really feel further support is required, express your concerns to the speech pathologist, who may be able to offer some professional help if just to reassure you. You can always phone at anytime if you are unsure of what to do or if you are concerned about your child's progress.

If your child is seeing a speech pathologist there are some general rules which apply to any type of therapy. Your role as parents is vital and speech and language therapy will only be successful if you are committed and directly involved. We always tell families who are about to start therapy that we cannot 'cure' the problem in one or even three sessions a week, it is up to the parents and child to practise and reinforce what is learnt as much as possible at home.

Your child spends a lot of hours at home with you, even if it doesn't seem like it! Home is also a natural communication environment where your child should feel comfortable when attempting new skills. So if you do want your child to progress quickly, it is important to carry out the recommended home activities. We can assure you that the effort is worth it.

If your child has a more severe speech problem, a speech pathologist may recommend increasing your use of gestures and teaching the child to use some gestures as a way of getting his message across. It is a common belief this will discourage your child's attempts to use verbal communication, however research has shown exactly the opposite is true. If we let the child use gestures in the short term, we are taking some pressure away from him to do what he finds hardest, that is, to talk. As he uses the gestures he will automatically start to attempt some of the words because he is feeling more confident. Your speech pathologist would guide you through this process.

Sometimes children's speech clarity is poor or they are unable to say certain sounds because they do not have good control over the muscles of their mouth. Occasionally this can't be improved upon, such as when it is due to neurological damage in cerebral palsy. However, some of the children we see benefit from incorporating oral exercises into their therapy program. You can make this a fun activity by pretending to be clowns making funny faces in the mirror. Make sure you join in to let your child see it is not threatening. Oral activities aim to refine the range of movements and also improve the control of these movements. Good strong lip closure is important for eating, drinking and talking. Some children can't make their lips rounded as in the sound 'oo'. Others can't stretch their tongue up towards their nose or point the tip of the tongue when asked. This affects their ability to produce clear speech sounds. So, have fun with your tongue and lips! The Mr Tongue game on page 49 in Chapter 3 is good fun. Some other suggestions are listed in the Oral Muscle Exercises on page 62.

ORAL MUSCLE EXERCISES

- Tightly close your lips around a straw.

- Stretch your lips as when you say 'eee'.

- Move your lips from the stretched 'eee' position to the wide open 'ah' position. Repeat this several times with exaggerated movements.

- Poke out your tongue and point the tip of it. Lick some icing sugar or peanut butter from a spoon with the pointed tongue tip.

- Poke out your tongue and move it from side to side in a steady controlled way.

- Lick your lips going all the way around the top lip and then all the way around the bottom lip in a steady controlled movement.

- Drag the tip of your tongue from behind your top teeth along the roof of your mouth. Does it tickle?

- Blow bubbles or a candle with rounded lips (as in the 'ooo' lip position).

- Blow bubbles or a candle as you say a *p* sound.

- Click your tongue like a horse.

Speech disorders

Speech disorders are characterised by unusual and atypical features which children retain as they mature. General progress in speech development is much slower when there is a disordered speech pattern.

The four most common speech disorders are explained below. You may be familiar with some of these terms.

PHONOLOGICAL DISORDER

A phonological disorder is characterised by problems understanding how the rules of sounds are used in speech. This often results in speech that is extremely difficult to understand. Many sounds may be omitted or substituted. These rules of speech sounds are investigated in Chapter 3. A child with this type of disorder may use rules typical of a much younger child or may have a pattern unique to them. It is possible that individual sounds can be produced accurately but not used at all in conversation. Some of the typical rule errors that occur include:

- quiet short sounds, *p*, *t* and *k*, are made into the louder partner that is *b*, *d* and *g*;
- sounds made by the back of the tongue in the mouth, *k* and *g*, may be produced by the tongue tip instead and become *t* and *d* respectively;
- all consonants on the end of words may be omitted.

A thorough evaluation and understanding of the child's rule pattern is essential before any therapy can be offered. Rather than working on an individual sound the speech pathologist may work on a group of sounds covered by a particular rule. The rules chosen will probably follow the normal developmental sequence.

DYSPRAXIA

Children with dyspraxia have problems organising and planning muscle movements, which can result in severely distorted speech. The child may find controlling oral muscle movement difficult even when speech is not required. All movement, including speed and accuracy may be affected. Even when a child has been taught how to produce individual sounds there is still the difficulty of linking the movement of one sound to the next to produce words.

DYSARTHRIA

Children with dysarthria have muscles that are very low in tone and do not function very well, resulting in poor control. Speech may be slow, jerky and slurred with varying degrees of individual speech sound errors. This is quite common in children with cerebral palsy.

CLEFT PALATE

A cleft palate is an opening in the soft palate and roof of the mouth, sometimes extending through the upper lip. Children born with a cleft palate are at risk of having speech and/or language problems associated with problems of the palate function, the use of incorrect patterns of tongue movement and even hearing loss. These children have speech which sounds nasal and they often overuse the back of their tongue which results in sounds being made in the wrong place. Surgery, orthodontics and speech therapy can help many of these children achieve adequate speech.

Be patient, as some severe speech problems require years of therapy. You might feel as if the weekly therapy is not bringing about changes quickly; sometimes it takes a while and then suddenly your child will show a big improvement overnight. It is also important to remember we may not notice the small improvements that happen day to day because we are too close to the situation and too used to the way our child speaks. Often parents will come back to therapy after a holiday and report on relatives commenting about 'how much your child's speech has improved'! If you're unsure at any time, ask your child's speech pathologist to specify the exact improvements she has noticed. Do remember there is always light at the end of the tunnel.

LANGUAGE DELAY AND DISORDERS
Language delay

As with speech delay, a language delay is when a child is progressing along normal pathways of development but at a slower rate. He may be using fewer words and shorter sentences than is expected for his age and as he gets older he may use immature grammar forms. It is alright for a two-year-old to say 'him' instead of 'he' but not when he is four or five. You might ask 'What difference does it make if he is ten months behind with his language?' Well, it can become significant if he is not given the opportunity to 'catch up' to his peers. Language and listening skills are crucial if he is to succeed at school, and children who start preschool with a delay in these skills are at an immediate disadvantage. He may not be able to follow the teacher's instructions

CHARACTERISTICS OF LANGUAGE DELAY

- At a young age, the child is behind or slower in the development of language.

- 'Normal' pattern of development is followed but at a slower rate.

- Understanding of language is usually near to age-appropriate level.

- Expressive language is mainly affected.

- Vocabulary (word) knowledge is less developed.

- Grammar errors used are typical of a younger child.

- Sentences are short and grammar simple compared to same-age children.

- Child may be quiet and withdrawn in a group and a poor listener.

- Less imagination evident in stories — often use repetitive themes and words.

- Level of abstract thinking and problem-solving may be less than his peers.

- Child may overgeneralise the names of things.

if she uses concepts that he is not familiar with and he may not be able to string words together in the correct order to form ideas and share at 'Show and Tell' time.

Children who use immature language may be teased and therefore become less willing to communicate; again this affects their play skills and their social interaction. There is also a large body of evidence indicating that even if your child does 'catch up' he will be at much greater risk of literacy problems once he gets to school. Recent statistics show that 10 to 15 per cent of two-year-olds are late talkers, that is, they are saying fewer than 50 words and/or using no word combinations. Law *et al* (2000) found that spontaneous remission occurred in up to 60 per cent of these children in the two- to three-year age group. You may well ask therefore 'Why bother doing anything about my two-year-old who's not saying much because he'll probably be in the 60 per cent who catch up spontaneously?' Well, even if your child does catch up spontaneously, just being a 'late talker' puts him at greater risk of having literacy problems at school. Of the 60 per cent in Law's study who showed spontaneous remission, more than 40 per cent had identifiable reading problems at age eight. In our view therefore it is worthwhile seeking advice.

If your child has been diagnosed with a language delay there are many useful ways you can help him to progress. Several of these techniques have already been explained in Chapter 2 in the age-related sections.

An important and ongoing task is to expand your child's vocabulary. Talk to him about everything and use new words over and over so he learns that one word can be used in a variety of contexts. Try to be precise in the words you use with your child; he will not improve if he constantly hears you say 'the thing' and 'the stuff'! Teach him the names of categories and the items that belong in each group.

'Can you tell me as many fruits you can think of?'
*'What furniture do we have in our house and which rooms
do they belong in?'*

Make sure you use lots of describing words (adjectives such as 'sticky', 'sharp', 'prickly'), as the more words he learns the more interesting will be his speech and later on his story writing. Make up personal picture storybooks about different categories; junk mail catalogues come in handy! Choose words around topics he likes or link it in with a holiday or weekend outing. It's amazing how many words you can think of to do with a topic if you put your mind to it. Use a kitchen timer and have a race against the clock to see how many words you can both think of.

Listening skills need to be a part of a language-delayed child's therapy program. Just because he can pass a hearing test doesn't mean he is automatically a good listener! Often these children are poor listeners because the language they are hearing is so much more complex than they understand or use themselves. Sometimes they have auditory memory problems and the message they just heard is lost. Further information on listening is included in Chapter 5.

In contrast to a language delay, some children have a more significant language problem known by a number of labels. These labels include **specific language impairment, language disorder** and **developmental language disorder.** There is ongoing debate in the speech pathology profession as to which label should be used. It currently depends on factors such as which State you work in, which Department you work in and which term is the 'in' one amongst academics in the field. What we do know is that a group of children exists which presents clinically with similar characteristics and whose progress is much slower than those of the same age with a language delay.

Language disorders

Some language disorders can be diagnosed quite early in childhood depending on the presenting group of problems. Other disorders become more evident as the child gets older and moves into preschool.

We have included in this section some information on types of disorders or disabilities that include language problems. No disorders are exclusive and unfortunately some children have more than one disorder. The definitions of these disorders vary from country to country and are often in dispute amongst professionals. Some disorders also sound very similar and it will take an experienced professional to make a correct diagnosis. The descriptions given are general guidelines only. If you feel your child may have a specific problem you can find more information from the references provided in 'Further reading for parents and carers'.

In our discussion of language-disordered children, we are only referring to those who have an isolated language disorder and otherwise average or above average intelligence. Children with an intellectual disability can also be language disordered but they require a different approach. Irrespective of the label used, we know that language-disordered children have very significant language difficulties

CHARACTERISTICS OF LANGUAGE DISORDER

- Following directions is difficult.

- Poor attention to spoken language and poor eye contact.

- Poor attention to tasks, your child is easily distracted and/or overactive.

- Lack of understanding of even simple concepts or words appropriate for his age.

- Good clarity of speech.

- Echoing or copying of the last words you say rather than responding appropriately.

- Giving responses which have no relationship to the topic of conversation or the questions asked.

- Very good at reciting by rote.

- Using language which is jumbled, with words omitted or put in the wrong place in the sentence.

- Poor, unimaginative play skills.

- Poor social skills as he does not understand sharing and turn-taking.

- Becomes upset with changes in routines.

which they do not grow out of and which affect their academic potential, no matter how bright they are according to intelligence tests. The language-disordered child does not learn language in the same developmental sequence as a language-delayed child does.

If your child is diagnosed with a language disorder, it is important he receives adequate and appropriate intervention. He will not respond to the conventional 'language stimulation' therapy. He will not learn language incidentally through everyday experiences but rather it will seem as if he needs to be taught everything separately.

Progress with these children depends on factors such as his overall intellectual ability, the type and amount of therapy he receives and the amount of practice work he does at home. Often a diagnosis is made based on the child's age and how slow his rate of progress is for his age. Therapy may go on for years, long after your child has started school. Unfortunately these language difficulties have a significant impact on your child's ability to learn in the classroom. All areas of the school curriculum require the child to listen, understand and express himself both verbally and in written form. It is very hard to listen in class if you don't understand what is being said or written. How can you do the maths problem if you didn't understand the teacher describing what 'subtract' means? Life for a young language-disordered child must be like being in a foreign country where you don't know the language. Have you ever tried watching a foreign film without subtitles? Do you know what they're saying?

Therapy for language disorders is very complex so it is vital that you have your child assessed and helped with appropriate therapy as soon as you feel there is a problem. A child with a language disorder is never too young to have help. The better his language skills are by the time he starts school, the less frustrating his school life will be.

Once a child has developed an understanding of the basic concepts of language and is speaking in sentences, parents often feel professional help is no longer required. But once he has the basics of how to communicate he then needs to learn to use his language effectively to solve problems, formulate solutions and understand the consequences of his actions etc. These pragmatic skills will influence his social skills as well as academic progress.

SEMANTIC PRAGMATIC DISORDER

It is possible to have a specific problem with *using* language appropriately, which is termed 'semantic pragmatic disorder'. For example, a child at a young age seemed to have a language impairment and was very slow to talk but then sentences, grammar and vocabulary suddenly developed so that on the surface he appeared to be speaking appropriately. However, there was something unusual about him and when you looked closely he still had a noticeable problem with how he used his language, that is, with his pragmatic skills. So at first the problem didn't seem any different from a language disorder but as the child got older the difficulties became more distinctive.

PERVASIVE DEVELOPMENTAL DISORDER

The American Psychiatric Association acknowledged that there are many people who don't quite meet the criteria to be diagnosed autistic but have some autistic tendencies. In the USA this group of problems is referred to as 'pervasive developmental disorder'. This term is beginning to be used outside the USA, and as parents you may come across this term as you are searching for information.

ASPERGER'S SYNDROME

In Australia some children can be diagnosed as having Asperger's syndrome. This is a milder form of autism and the child may present as very unusual or eccentric. There is impairment in the understanding of the intricacies of daily interaction. This leads to poor social skills, demonstrating problems with pragmatic skills that are discussed in Chapter 2 on pages 39–42. Their use of facial expressions and their understanding of facial expressions used by others is limited or nonexistent. Speech can be perfect structurally but can be pedantic and stereotyped in nature. These children usually have an area or theme of special interest, which keeps recurring throughout the course of every activity. As with autism (see below), children with Asperger's are comforted by routine and can be quite distressed by any changes. Motor coordination is often poor, resulting in clumsy movement and an unusual gait and posture.

AUTISM

Autism is a more severe disorder which prevents a child from processing and using language, and social and sensory information in an appropriate way. It is usually diagnosed within the first two or three years of life. Children with autism appear withdrawn from other people and may not appear to respond to other children at all. The symptoms may be different, with some eventually speaking adequately while others may not speak at all. Often the children go through a period of 'echolalia'. This is when they repeat the exact words they have just heard spoken. Changes in routine, loud noises or lots of activity may cause distress. There may be repetitive or stereotyped behaviour.

For many children the cause of speech and language impairment is unknown: the speech and language pattern doesn't relate to hearing, intellectual ability or any autistic tendencies. For some children there is a genetic component with a family history of speech, language or learning difficulties.

Regardless of whether or not the cause is identified, or whether a specific diagnosis has been made, therapy programs are designed based on each child's unique set of strengths and weaknesses. Goals should be small and obtainable with everyone working together on the same aim: to maximise your child's language and learning potential so he can communicate as effectively as possible with those around him.

5 Hearing and listening problems

Hearing and listening play a vital role in the development of communication skills.

Hearing is the physical act of the ear receiving sound and sending the 'noise' to the brain for analysis. We need to be able to hear adequately to listen properly, however, it is possible to have excellent hearing but poor listening ability. Listening is being able to pay attention and remember the important parts of a message, then being able to retrieve this information at a later time.

Once the brain receives the sound, it has to be sorted out, organised and processed. In other words, the brain has to make sense of the different sounds it has heard. When you are playing in the garden with your children there is a variety of noises surrounding you. There might be conversations, squeals of excitement, a swing creaking, a sprinkler on, cars passing by, children in a swimming pool next door, a dog barking and many more noises all occurring simultaneously. The brain organises these noises, distinguishes the background sounds and the important sounds for us to listen and respond to. Despite all this noise, when the doorbell rings immediate attention transfers to this sound. Your child might run to the door knowing that this sound should not be ignored.

This chapter will explain the hearing process and the auditory skills that are necessary for language and learning development.

HEARING

The hearing process involves four separate parts, each of which plays a crucial role. The *outer ear*, on the outside of the head collects the sound and sends it to the *middle ear*. The middle ear consists of the eardrum or tympanic membrane and three tiny linked bones called the ossicles.

The eardrum vibrates on receiving the sound and passes it down the chain of bones to the inner ear. The middle ear also contains the eustachian tube which connects the middle ear to the throat and is the mechanism by which pressure is balanced within the ear. The *inner ear* is responsible for controlling, balancing and transferring the sound

THE HEARING PROCESS

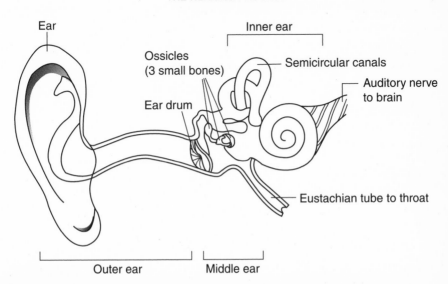

Ear

Inner ear

Ossicles
(3 small bones)

Semicircular canals

Auditory nerve
to brain

Ear drum

Eustachian tube to throat

Outer ear   Middle ear

DEVELOPMENT OF HEARING

Newborn A newborn baby gives a startle reflex to a loud sound, flinging their arms and legs out wide.

2–3 months Babies are less startled and responses are milder.

4–6 months Loud sounds result in a slight movement of the eyes or a stilling of all movement. Enjoys a variety of sound and music.

6–9 months Begins to locate the source of the sound and will turn to find it. He will respond to his name and to familiar sounds and voices.

10–15 months Responds to simple things that you say. May say single words.

15–18 months Can easily locate and identify the source of sound. Responds to simple commands and is developing a wide spoken vocabulary.

---

waves into nerve signals. From the inner ear sound is carried down the nervous system, which has to make sense of the sound waves it receives, to the brain. The central auditory system receives this information from each ear and has to make sense of the sound waves that it receives.

Types of hearing loss

There are two kinds of hearing loss: a conductive hearing loss and a sensorineural hearing loss. A **conductive** hearing loss is a blockage in the transmission of sound waves to the inner ear resulting in everything sounding muffled. This is the more common type of hearing loss and the one we encounter with preschoolers who have recurrent middle ear infections (also known as *otitis media*). A child prone to these infections has fluctuations in his ability to hear clearly, so it is vital to have his hearing checked for any problems. Even though the hearing loss is usually temporary and eliminated once the fluid is removed from the middle ear, it can affect a child's speech and language development. A child will typically say a word the way he hears it, so if your speech sounds muffled to him, the chances are he will say it incorrectly. For example, if he thinks he heard you say 'see' as 'thee', he will most likely say 'thee'. The longer his hearing loss lasts, the more habitual these sound errors will become, making remediation more difficult.

A **sensorineural** hearing loss occurs because of damage to the inner ear or the nerve pathways from the inner ear to the brain. The result is a permanent loss of hearing acuity. The information below on Sounds and Hearing shows that it is not only the loudness levels at which a person hears information that are important but also the frequencies or pitches which can be heard. Loudness levels are measured in decibels (dB) and frequencies are measured in cycles per

---

SOUNDS AND HEARING

0–20dB Normal range of hearing. All speech sounds are heard appropriately.

20–30dB Slight hearing loss may be caused by ear infections. Vowels and most consonants in speech are heard without any amplification. Mild auditory problems and so treatment may be required. The test results are useful to a speech pathologist.

30–40dB Mild hearing loss. Mild language, speech and learning problems. Requires a hearing aid and specialist support. Uses lip reading.

40–60dB Moderate hearing loss. Misses most speech at normal conversational level. Speech, language and learning problems. Will require special classroom attention.

60–95dB Severe hearing loss. Will probably require special schooling.

95 dB Profoundly deaf. Severe speech and language problems. Needs treatment and special education.

---

second (cps) or hertz (Hz). This information is important to parents and speech pathologists because all speech sounds are produced at a particular decibel and frequency range. So, if a child has a 50dB hearing loss no sound is detected below 50dB and between 500 and 4000Hz, he would have difficulty hearing and therefore copying the sounds *r, p, g, k* and *t.*

Identifying a hearing loss

Sometimes the child's response or lack of response to sound and the way he communicates causes concern. This may not necessarily be symptomatic of a hearing problem, but if there are difficulties with speech and language skills it is important to check the possibility of a hearing loss. Early detection and treatment is very important to prevent or reduce communication problems. Any suspicion of a hearing loss should be taken seriously and warrants testing. No child or baby is too young to be tested. If their hearing proves to be normal, no harm has been done.

The ear can be examined externally by a doctor who checks for visual signs of inflammation or blockage. But clinical symptoms alone are not enough to rule out the possibility of a hearing loss.

In very young children concerns may be strong enough to warrant evaluation by auditory brainstem response. Three electrodes are placed on the baby's head. A sound is made in the baby's ear by headphone and the brain's response is recorded.

Audiometric assessment is the procedure which many parents are familiar with and your child's hearing may be screened in this way prior to entry into preschool. A qualified person, preferably an audiologist, should carry out the testing. To assess your child, sound is presented into each ear through headphones. Pitch and volume can be varied to measure your child's hearing threshold. This is measured in decibels. Your child's cooperation is essential as he has to indicate when he has heard the sound. If you are sitting in the room with your child while testing is in progress make sure that you don't give away any clues that you have heard a sound otherwise the evaluation will be inaccurate. A bright child is more than capable of picking up clues

SYMPTOMS OF HEARING LOSS

1   Inattention, restlessness.

2   Failure to follow instructions.

3   Frequent requests for information to be repeated. Waits to observe other children first.

4   Watching the speaker's face closely.

5   Turning the head to one side when listening.

6   Misunderstanding of instructions and directions, with inappropriate answers.

7   Inability to cope with more than one item of information at a time.

8   Mispronounces or omits certain consonants when talking.

9   Difficulties in locating the source of sound. Even a young baby turns his head towards his parent's voice. By six months he will turn his head in the direction from which a sound is coming.

10   In school-age children, daydreaming or perhaps a deterioration in their work.

11   Reluctance to participate in activities requiring oral communication.

12   Increase or decrease in loudness of the voice.

13   Increased or decreased tolerance of loud sounds.

14   Ringing in the ears.

15   Medical indications such as mouth breathing, earache and colds.

Source: Early Childhood Services, Department of Education, Employment and Training, South Australia.

from your facial expressions and body language when a sound has been played.

In 'impedance audiometry' a small metal 'stick' attached to a computer is placed inside the ear to measure air pressure. This test is particularly good at picking up any sign of fluid in the middle ear or any type of eustachian tube dysfunction.

These tests do not take very long to administer but are important for finding or ruling out possible causes of problems. Most people are aware a severe hearing loss has grave consequences for the acquisition of spoken language. But mild to moderate levels of hearing loss can have a profound influence on the development of articulation, vocabulary and grammar. For normal speech development sound needs to be loud enough and heard frequently enough during the critical period of language learning.

Only if a hearing loss is identified can the appropriate treatment be initiated. In the case of severe and/or recurrent middle ear infection (glue ear) a course of antibiotics may be prescribed or grommets (small tubes) may be inserted into the eardrum to enable fluid to drain away. With a permanent hearing loss the use of a hearing aid may be recommended together with therapy and teaching support from a speech pathologist and a specialist teacher.

LISTENING

Some children can technically hear but the brain has difficulty sorting out the sounds it received, that is, the brain has trouble processing auditory information. Many of us may believe learning to listen happens naturally in much the same way as we may believe learning to talk does. Even though listening is not taught as a formal school subject, we do need to be guided in the use of this skill right from our early days as a newborn. Studies have shown that between 50 and 75 per cent of a student's classroom time is spent listening. They listen to the teacher, to other students and to audio materials such as tapes, CDs and videos. So we can easily see why a day in the classroom is difficult for a child who has trouble listening.

Most of us probably think mainly of ears when we think of listening.

However, we really use our whole body when we listen. We need our ears to hear the sound and block out any background noise. We need our eyes so we can look at the speaker. We need our brain to listen so we can make sense of and think about what is being said. We listen with our mouth by being quiet and not interrupting. We also listen with our hands and feet by keeping them still and not fidgeting.

Developing good listening skills

Your young child loves to copy you, so the best way to teach him good listening skills is for you to model good listening skills to him.

Show an interest When your child is very young show an interest in what he is saying. Whether you like it or not, your child will know if he has your attention by the way you reply or don't reply to him.

Listen and look Listen patiently and give him time to talk. Forget about the telephone and other distractions, unless the house is about to burn down! Don't interrupt him; what he is saying is important to him even if it's not important to you. Look at him while he is talking and encourage him to look at you. Maintaining eye contact during conversation is just as important for the child as it is for the adult.

Minimise noise Keep background noise to a minimum. It is very hard to give a conversation your full attention if you are competing with a television or other noisy children.

Read books Reading books is a great way to encourage good listening. Ask your child questions about the content as you read it.

Encourage imitating Have your child imitate simple clapping sequences.

Record his voice Tape-record your child's voice as he recites a nursery rhyme and then play it back to him a few days later. Does he recognise his own voice?

Give instructions through games Play games where you give your child an instruction for him to carry out. Gradually increase the length and complexity of the instructions according to his language level. You can do this by involving the body. 'Go under your chair and then clap your hands.' You can give instructions with toys or magnetic shapes 'Put the train under the bridge and put the horse on the bridge'; and later on you can use pencil and paper to draw a picture, 'Draw a little circle in the middle of the paper. Now draw a line from the top of the circle to the top of the paper.' This is also a fun way of improving your child's memory.

Make conversation Encourage your child to participate in family conversations. Let him talk about his day and his activities.

There is a range of auditory skills that are necessary to really listen properly. These include:

- awareness that sounds are different;
- localising where different sounds are coming from;
- paying attention;
- discriminating between very similar sounds, especially for speech, such as between *f* and *th*;
- remembering information that you have been told;
- sequencing the information into a logical order.

Problems with auditory skills can be mild or severe, affect only one area or a combination of the skills.

Developing auditory memory and sequencing

We can remember details presented in a variety of ways. It may be something you felt, smelt, saw or experienced as well as heard. The more fully you participated the more likely you are to remember. It is easier to remember the way to a friend's house if you have driven the car there before and less likely if you were a passenger in the car. Auditory memory is particularly important in the academic learning process. Classrooms become less 'hands on' as children get older and rely more on verbal interaction.

If your child can listen appropriately and has adequate language skills, he should be able to remember information he hears. This may be words or names or complete instructions. As he becomes better at remembering he will also learn that some information needs to be remembered in a particular sequence. A number of techniques are given here to help develop your child's auditory memory.

Give short instructions Keep your instructions short to start with and gradually increase how many things your child needs to remember, by using the activities described in the preceding section. Start with one thing and later expect him to remember two, then three and so on.

Play games Play a memory game such as 'I went shopping and I bought some apples.' Your child then has a turn and has to say what you said and add one more item, 'I went shopping and bought apples and ice cream'. Continue taking turns, adding one item until he can't remember anymore. Use activities or outings relevant to your child, such as 'When we went to the zoo we saw ...'

Play 'Simon Says' using simple then more complex requests, for example, 'Touch your nose, touch your head, sit down.' Don't worry if he doesn't get the idea of the 'Simon Says' part initially as the main idea is for him to complete the actions.

Remember shopping items Ask your child to remind you about one shopping-list item, for example, as you leave home say 'I want you to remind me to buy honey', then when you enter the supermarket ask, 'Do you remember what we had to buy?'

To make the shopping-list game easier with your younger child, use your fingers as a visual reminder to count the number of parts of the instruction. For example, 'What do I need? I need honey (count one finger) and juice (count second finger).' Encourage him to use his fingers to count items.

Ask questions Ask questions about your instruction, for example, 'Where are you going to put your shoes?'

Use inflection in your voice Use rhythm and 'music' in your voice to help rote memory tasks such as number sequences and nursery rhymes and later spelling of longer words. Can your child say his telephone number?

Take messages Encourage your child to take messages between Mum and Dad. Keep them short at first but gradually require an answer to come back.

Create a picture If your child has difficulty remembering encourage him to shut his eyes and create a picture in his mind of the activity then ask him to describe the picture he has created.

DEVELOPING AUDITORY DISCRIMINATION

Auditory discrimination is the ability to perceive or distinguish differences between the sounds we hear. This can relate to simple sounds such as those in our environment, for example, running water through to more complex individual speech sounds and words. Can he hear the difference between a vacuum cleaner and a kettle boiling? Can he hear the difference between 'bear' and 'beer' or between 'shore' and 'door'? Problems in this area can result in poorly developed vocabulary knowledge and a delay in receptive language skills. If he has problems in sound-symbol association or perceiving the presence or absence of sounds in a word, he will be at a great disadvantage when trying to read and spell. It will also affect his use of grammar: he may not be able to hear the 's' on the end of 'cars' to indicate there is more than one.

It is important to mention that some children have difficulty discriminating speech sounds produced by others while others have more difficulty discriminating their own speech. Here are some ideas to help develop your child's auditory discrimination.

Differentiate sounds Very early games can include listening for and talking about the sounds heard in everyday activities inside or outside the home. When you are cooking highlight the different sounds such as the frying pan hissing, the kettle boiling, the fridge motor rumbling and the toast popping up.

Use kitchen items such as saucepan lids, spoons, rice in a container (with a very good lid!), bells and ice-cream containers. Take turns to close your eyes while the other person makes a sound with one of the items. Open your eyes. Can you guess which one made the sound? Was it a loud quick drumbeat with the spoon and lid? Or was it a long quiet roll of the rice container? You can also do this with some toy musical instruments.

Describe sounds Describe a sound according to its volume, pitch and duration. Is the sound loud or soft? Is it high or low pitched? Is it a long or short sound?

Use rhyme to differentiate sounds in words Having your child choose which words rhyme and then thinking of his own word that rhymes with the given word is a wonderful way to teach the discrimination skills required in the classroom.

The older preschool child will be able to listen to two or three words and decide whether they have the same or a different sound at the beginning, the end and in the middle, for example, 'dog' and 'dig'. Do they have the same first sound? middle sound? end sound? Many preschool activity books have such tasks included, otherwise just draw your own pictures!

Count syllables and find 'silly' words Being able to count the number of syllables in a word and being able to discriminate an incorrect, or 'silly' word, in a sentence are also important skills and can be practised in a fun way at home. Your child will love silly sentences such as 'The cat barked as it climbed the tree' or 'Daddy wore his bathers to bed.'

Specific auditory problems

Sometimes children present with a whole range of auditory problems. These problems sometimes co-exist with other disabilities such as dyslexia or language disorder. However, it is possible for the auditory difficulties to present as the main problem.

Children with speech and language impairment often present with other problems with their listening, attention and other auditory skills. They might not have a clearly identifiable disorder like those mentioned below but problems with auditory-based skills are still interfering with development.

CENTRAL AUDITORY PROCESSING DISORDER (CAPD/APD)

A diagnosis of CAPD/APD should be made on the basis of audiological tests during which the child undertakes various listening tasks in a soundproof room. The tests are often initiated by teachers or speech pathologists, noticing a child is struggling with listening tasks even though he is capable of concentrating on a wide range of other activities. In particular, the child may be distracted by background noise — perhaps something as minor as the air conditioner. They might also notice the child tires easily during listening tasks, forgets or is confused by what he is told. There could also be associated comprehension and reading difficulties.

In these circumstances the child would learn more effectively by using visual methods rather than auditory input. Also when the noisy classroom is proving disastrous, short periods working quietly one on one can be highly effective. Unfortunately the child with listening difficulties does need to learn to cope in the classroom. An assessment will help identify ways of modifying the school environment to improve his learning.

ATTENTION DEFICIT DISORDER (ADD)

Children with ADD can be confused with CAPD but usually they also present with a group of behavioural difficulties. Some children, but not all, are extremely active as well and therefore have attention deficit hyperactivity disorder (ADHD). Their minds and/or their bodies are working extremely quickly. Everything seems to distract them.

A child with ADD can be a major problem within the classroom because he is unable to stay focused for a reasonable period of time. The child may be impulsive and disorganised as well which doesn't help his social skills. He may often call out in the classroom and can be disruptive to the other children trying to concentrate and learn. Even having a conversation can be confusing for the child as the topic may chop and change or he may interrupt the person speaking at the most inappropriate times. This reduced ability to concentrate and stay focused may also lead to listening and language problems.

6 **Learning to talk from other sources**

THE ROLE OF PLAY

It has always been acknowledged that play is fun. However, until the beginning of the last century, it was also thought that play was a waste of time. It was accepted that young children spent their time playing because they were not capable of doing anything more useful. Once children went to school they were expected to work, and play was then kept for holidays or when work was completed. But in fact, play *is* your child's work!

We now know that play is the most important activity a child can do from birth to about seven or eight years of age. Play is more than a means of passing time or keeping children occupied. It is the way young children learn just about everything: about themselves, their environment and the people around them, and about growing up. When you watch your child play, you will see him practise old skills as well as learn new ones. He will learn to be creative, solve problems, get along with other people and control his body as he explores toys.

Because your child learns so many skills from playing, it is an essential part of his development. Physical skills are developed through movement as your child learns to reach, grasp, crawl, run, climb and balance; fine motor dexterity develops as he handles and manipulates objects in play; and social and emotional skills develop through positive play experiences. Your child learns to cooperate, share, negotiate, take turns and play by the rules. Whether we like it or not, imaginative play is the way your child will learn some social roles and rules.

By feeling successful and competent in their play, children will forge ahead in their confidence and self-esteem. Sharing play experiences with your child will also help strengthen bonds between you. Language develops as your child plays and interacts with others. Starting with simple cooing games, your child's language will gradually move through the stages of development to a sophisticated level of telling stories and jokes. Most children want to learn to talk, and later to read, and write and many of the toys they play with at an earlier age help them to do this. There is no question that a child who has had good play opportunities and a wide variety of play experiences will have an obvious advantage when learning to talk, read and write.

As adults, we need to remind ourselves that the many hours spent playing are really laying the foundation for all intellectual activity. Free play has an important role but as parents we must also remember that we can help our child to realise his full learning potential by modifying and developing play activities. Research clearly shows that the most creative children are those who have had adults involved in their play. The richest play takes place when you, as the parent, take an active role and play alongside your child, rather than just providing the toys and supervising the activity.

We're sure some of you feel strange getting down on the floor to play with your infant. After all, it might look too 'childish'! But if you are having fun with your child does it matter? Following are some ways of joining in with your child's play.

Observe Watch your child closely to determine his level of skill and his favourite activities.

Follow Join in with your child and play at his level. When appropriate, you can add some complexity to the activity, but it is important to your child's confidence that he is in control and can determine the direction of the play.

Be creative Discover how many different ways you can use a toy with your child. Children bring energy and imagination to their play to help them foster creativity. Rediscover the child within you.

Have fun Playtime is not test time. If you are relaxed and enjoying yourself, your child can't help but relax and have fun with you. Before you know it they won't want to play with you any more, so enjoy it while it lasts.

TYPES OF PLAY

Each child is unique and develops at his own pace, however, if you watch your child as he grows, you will see that his play changes. As your child becomes more skilled and experienced his play becomes more diverse, creative and sophisticated. These different stages of play can be categorised in the following way.

Exploratory play

In the first year, your infant learns about his environment by using all five senses: sight, touch, hearing, smell and taste. Exploratory play, which begins at about three months, lets your child observe and discover objects in his environment. Objects arouse curiosity and a desire to learn and your child will use all his senses to find out about them. Toys will provide a small baby with opportunities to learn about size, shape, sound, texture and how things work. Finger play is important for eye–hand coordination, seeing where sounds come from, understanding the permanence of objects and learning to appreciate time and space.

Imitative play

Imitative play begins at about nine months and reflects what your child sees and hears around him, particularly in everyday situations. Your

WHAT CAN PLAY DO?

- Play has many purposes for a young child. It is a serious business which should never be frowned upon by adults.

- Play allows your child to develop new skills through observation, exploration and discovery.

- Play allows your child to practise skills he has already learnt.

- Play develops language understanding, concept formation and language expression. Children seldom play silently, even when alone. They are constantly talking. It gives them practice in conveying, reporting and discovering information. It can be used to describe incidents and tell stories. Play enables questions to be asked.

- Play is fun.

- Play can relieve boredom and frustration and allow for the release of physical energy.

- Play can let your child experience and express feelings of achievement, failure, satisfaction, pleasure and frustration.

- Play allows your child to act out other people's roles and helps develop a gender identity.

- Play helps children form friendships and gain cooperation. It also allows your child to learn to cope by himself and with other people.

- Play allows your child to be creative and independent. The level of creativity and discovery will invariably match the child's environment.

child will love to copy you so you will need to provide constant 'models'. By providing them with safe and similar replicas of the objects you use, you can let them participate in seemingly mundane chores in an enjoyable way. You are setting the scene for them so they can learn how to carry out certain actions, and later on they will understand why these actions are carried out.

Your one-year-old relishes physical play. He moves busily within his environment, walking, climbing, pushing and riding. All this play helps his physical development. He will learn to control his body better and coordinate his movements. Once independent, he is free to explore the world around him. So, let him crawl, roll, jump and climb as long as it's safe.

Constructive play

Constructive play begins around 18 months and enables your child to participate in an activity that results in an end product, such as building a tower with blocks. It is important for developing eye–hand coordination and memory. This type of play provides the perfect opportunity for learning about the size, shape, texture, weight and colour of objects. As well as a strong interest in manipulating objects, busy toddlers also like problem-solving with objects. They like sorting and fitting toys and puzzles.

Imaginative and make-believe play

By the time your child is two years-old, he will love imaginative and make-believe play. He loves being dramatic. In this type of play, children will use objects or gestures to represent other objects or events that are not present. Imaginative play is full of make-believe, fantasy and role-play. It is vital in language and social development. At this stage children are becoming more social. They become more interested in playing with each other instead of playing alone. 'Let's pretend' games prepare your child for the many situations and relationships he will encounter later on. Values and attitudes are developed through fantasy play also. Children will use play food, appliances and utensils, pretend money and cash registers, and play furniture and dress-up clothes to imitate what they have seen in the adult world around them.

Role-playing helps your child learn to understand others. If he is to understand others, he must have the chance to put himself in another's place.

Imaginative play also encourages creativity. The richer and more varied your child's experiences, the more he will have to act out. Our children have always spent a lot of time 'going on trips' in their play. They used to pack their bags, write out their airline tickets and list what they wanted to do while away. They would even take the oxygen mask from the toy doctor's kit in their bag just in case the plane crashed! Visitors and preschool staff used to be amazed at the detailed content of their language when discussing, for instance, the buffalo of Canada and the humid weather in Singapore. They were fortunate enough to have travelled alot as toddlers and it has always been a significant part of their play. One of them now writes long stories at school about the experiences she remembers from her holidays as a preschooler.

The growing complexity of play at this preschooler stage signals your child's increased capacity to think and use language. More complex thinking means more complex play and vice-versa. Visualisation and memory skills can be improved at this stage by imaginative play. The introduction of electronic toys, word and matching games, and board games are important at this age.

Games with rules

Games with rules become more frequent by the time your child is starting school. To play such games, your child needs to be able to share and take turns as well as be able to follow instructions and discuss the outcome of the game. Such games allow your child to practise language skills, and learn the social skills of winning and losing.

Board games, table-top sports games, marbles and craft kits also help children develop both social and solitary play skills as well. Using craft and science kits, children can start examining and experimenting with the world around them. Children often start collections or hobbies at this stage. We remember spending hours collecting and sorting stamps from around the world and it certainly teaches you the names of countries that some people have never heard of! One of our children now enjoys stamp collecting and it is definitely a good activity for rainy days. These games and hobbies also help their reading skills. In fact their whole world changes as they learn to read and write. Once the ticket-writing starts, you might find yourself 'invited' to many concerts — we have spent hundreds of hours listening to 'Kylie' and watching our children sing and dance. As such important audience members there is no way we are allowed to even leave our seat to answer the phone! We even have to pay for the ticket sometimes! Many of the electronic toys and games for this age group are labelled 'educational' because they are designed so skills relating to language concepts, reading and numbers can be practised.

This is a very physical stage with lots of games involving bikes, scooters, Rollerblades (and helmet!) and balls. Quieter games such as marbles, jacks, dominoes and cards are also popular.

Even though more time is spent playing in groups at this stage, children also enjoy playing by themselves. By now children are also very aware of gender stereotypes and know exactly what girls and boys are supposed to do. Often girls play with girls and boys play with boys. Girls will play 'mothers and babies' while boys will play with transport and construction sets. It is important to encourage children to change these stereotypes and let them know that it's okay to do so. Some friends thought it strange that our girls loved playing with the train set and constructing Lego ships, but they also loved, and still love, their dolls!

USING TOYS TO TEACH TALKING

When buying, choosing or making a toy, think about your child's level of language. How many words can he say? Is he at the single word or three-word phrase level? Look at the particular toy and think about what words you could model and encourage your child to copy while playing with it.

Let's look at a few toys and activities that are popular with toddlers and see what words you could teach.

BUILDING BLOCKS

- Blocks can represent many things such as people, cars and trains.
- Blocks can be used to teach number, colour and shape concepts.
- Specific concepts to practise include numbers, colours, same and different.
- Other words to model include 'more', 'on top', 'fall down', 'up' and 'down'.

A typical conversation with a two-year-old could go as follows:

As you place a block on the tower, you say: *'Look, more blocks. Your turn, ask mummy for more.'*

Child says *'More'* as he takes it.

As he places it on the tower you can say: *'One more, on top, red block.'* You ask: *'Want more?'*

Child says: *'More Mum'*.

'Good talking' you say reinforcing his nice asking.

As he places this block on the tower, you can say: *'Look, tall tower, lots of blocks. Let's count them. One, two, three . . . '*

Encourage your child to join in with the counting and then when he gets to the top say: *'Let's knock it down now. Are you ready? You knock them. Ready, set, go'*.

As they come tumbling down say: *'O-oh, crash. Blocks fall down!'*

PUZZLES

- Children love doing puzzles over and over and therefore you have lots of scope for teaching new words.
- Ask your child 'Where's . . . ?'
- Child asks for 'More' when he's ready to fit another piece.
- Other words to model include 'here' and 'there', 'in there' and 'in the hole'.
- Hold up a choice of two pieces and ask your child the name of the one he wants next.

This last suggestion is a very powerful way of encouraging a child to talk and it is a technique often used with children who have delayed language.

As your child takes the puzzle pieces out of the form board, put some of them on your lap. Let him put in a few pieces first, maybe naming them as he goes. Then hold up two puzzle pieces and ask 'Which one do you want to put in next, ball or plane?' Encourage the child to choose by naming the piece. If he is still at a single-word stage, accept 'ball' but if he can say short phrases why not encourage him to say 'I want the ball' or 'Ball please.'

BUBBLE BLOWING

- This is a fun and cheap activity.
- Incorporate words such as 'more', 'pop', 'all gone', 'bubbles' and 'no more'.
- Remember, always talk with your child when playing together and give him time to respond and talk.

Having fun without toys

Toys are the tools children use in their play. Toys can be purchased or they can be made at home; virtually anything a child can play with safely can be used as a toy. It could be a musical toy from the store or pots from the kitchen cupboard or even wrapping paper and ribbon from a present. Children will find all sorts of creative ways to use just about anything. Art and craft activities do not have to be put on hold until kindergarten. You probably already have most of the things you need. Don't throw out anything!

How do we know what toy to buy? We have often heard a frustrated parent ask this as they wander around a toy department of a large store. What factors might we consider when purchasing a toy?

When it comes to choosing a toy, safety, durability and usability are key factors. Age specifications are there for a reason: to help you decide on appropriate toys for a child of that particular age. As well as considering the product, it is also important to consider the child, his personality and his behaviour and reaction to other toys you've seen him with. Also, all children have different interests and hobbies. It is important to remember that each child is unique and develops at his own pace, therefore use the age labels as guides and, above all else, use common sense.

To determine the age labels for toys, toy makers follow age-grading guidelines comprising four main criteria:

- The ability of a child to physically manipulate and play with the features of a toy.
- The ability of a child to understand how to use a toy.
- The child's play needs and interests at different developmental levels.
- The safety aspects of the toy itself.

The group responsible for these guidelines is The Australian Toy Standard (AS1647) established by Standards Australia.

Remember, however, that toys, either bought or homemade are not always necessary, and you can have just as much fun without them. Here are some suggestions for play with and without toys for each age group.

NEWBORN

- Hold him close in front of you so he can look straight at you. Rock him gently.
- Have a conversation with him. Let him take turns with you by slightly nodding his head, moving his eyes and mouth.

BABIES: BIRTH TO ONE YEAR

Experts now agree that even babies benefit from a variety of toys. Well-selected toys at this age allow the baby to learn about size, texture, shape, sound and how things work. Rattles and squeaky toys are best and bright colours are generally more appealing. Babies love looking at board books filled with bright pictures of familiar objects. Blocks, stacking toys, nesting cups, balls and push-pull toys are great for a baby once they are sitting and crawling. Although you may become bored with the same rattle, remember babies love repetition! You can use these toys in the following ways.

- Encourage him to copy you blowing bubbles or blinking deliberately. He may even make noises as if he's talking back to you.
- Hide a toy he's been following and then ask 'Where's it gone?' Make it reappear and say 'There it is.'
- Have a mobile and some hitting toys around. Cotton reels, silver foil and ribbons blow well in the breeze and you can tie these on to a wire coat hanger.
- Play 'Peep-bo'.
- Let him touch you and pull your hair. Tickle him.
- Encourage him to splash in the bath and swim, if he likes it.
- Vary physical games from being held under the arms and gently swung, to clapping hands and a noisy rough-and-tumble.

- Make your own sound makers using rice in pots as rattles. Banging pots with wooden spoons is noisy and great fun.
- Play 'Pat-a-cake'.
- Sing 'Row the boat' and pretend to row as you hold baby's fingers.
- Play 'Round and round the garden' and 'This little piggy'.
- Let him copy you building towers and making them fall down. Use yoghurt tubs or small boxes. Decorate them with contact or let your child paste pictures on them.
- Encourage your infant to copy you by tapping his lips, waving, clapping and banging hands on the table.
- Let him stare at his reflection in a mirror.
- Initiate games where he offers things to you and you give them back.
- Crawl around together during exploring games.

INFANTS: ONE TO TWO YEARS

A toddler is busy and needs toys for active physical play. They like to walk, ride, push and climb. A tricycle or a wagon to ride is handy as is a rocking horse to sit on. Toddlers love the outdoors so a sandpit with digging toys as well as large balls and maybe a wading pool are all good fun at this stage. Cuddly toys as well as a wooden train and an abacus are useful. Toddlers also love following and catching bubbles so a bottle of bubble mixture will always be handy. Remember you can make your own mixture. In a large container, place one and a half cups of water. Add half a cup of dishwashing detergent and half a cup of glycerin. Stir gently. Store the mixture in a well-sealed jar. You can also add food colouring if you wish.

Children start to enjoy make-believe play nearer to their second birthday. Create a box of dress-up clothes. Use play food (or your own empty packets) and plastic utensils and set up a shop. Puzzles and other types of sorting and fitting toys will be appreciated. Puzzles are an expensive purchase and children like to move on to a new challenge and not just repeat the same puzzle over and over, so try borrowing puzzles from a toy library. Below are more ideas.

- Encourage your child to copy you (washing up) and help you (sweeping the floor). Use a real telephone. Telephone companies often give away old handsets, so it's worth making some enquiries.
- Make games out of routines such as getting dressed, or putting away the shopping. Sing songs to make it more fun: 'This is the way we carry the bags', 'This is where we put the cheese'. Make up your own versions for any situation.
- Play hide-and-seek by hiding objects around the room and finding them together.
- Play 'Ring-a-ring-a-roses' and musical chairs.
- Have fun at a playground. Jump in a pile of autumn leaves, feed the ducks and count the seagulls.
- Make homemade books including a 'Me Book' about your child's activities, family and friends.

TODDLERS: TWO TO THREE YEARS

Toddlers love musical instruments so keep at hand a supply of tambourines, drums, bells and CDs around. Children love to have their own little tape recorder so they can carry their music around and also tape their own singing. Nursery rhymes should be sung frequently to your toddler. Books are always a hit and more detailed information about books for children will be dealt with in Chapter 7. This age group especially likes lift-the-flap books.

Craft activities are in demand at this age. Make your own Playdough, which is cheaper than buying it all the time. Your child will love helping you 'cook' it! Have pastry cutters ready and whole stories can be made by just creating a few Playdough shapes and characters. Pencils, paper and paints are popular and good rainy-day activities. Take a plastic bag when you go walking and collect leaves, feathers, sticks and make a collage when you get home. A cubby house will provide hours of fun and exploration. A cubby house outdoors is great but remember children will also love a homemade one. Use your imagination with sheets and towels and a table and it's amazing what you can create. The pet dog might also love this game!

As well as swings and other climbing structures, another active game is playing skittles. You can buy them but why not make your own? We collected ten plastic bottles and then our children helped paint them and decorate them with stickers. They love knocking down the skittles and then chasing the ball. Each skittle was painted with one of the main colours so it was a good way of teaching colour naming. 'Which ones will you knock down next?' Create your own fishing game by making paper fish with paper clips on the end. Make a rod with a little magnet and see how many fish you can catch. You could paint a piece of cardboard blue for a pond. Children love this. Again you can teach colours and also numbers: 'How many red fish did you catch?'

PRESCHOOLERS: THREE TO FIVE YEARS

Imaginative play and the world of make-believe are high on the agenda for this age group. So, keep up your supply of dress-ups as well as props for their pretend worlds. Toys, furniture and boxes can all be used as props. Farms, doll houses, shops, garages and a puppet theatre are useful. You can make your own puppets from old socks and act out fairy tales such as *Goldilocks and the Three Bears.*

Hand skills are improving rapidly at this stage, so continue expanding the use of playdough and other craft activities. Construction sets and more complex puzzles will stimulate their minds. Some children at this age are learning to read and write so provide them with the appropriate play equipment to encourage this. Always have books, pencils and paper around. Let them 'write' your shopping list or write tickets for their puppet show. Children love a blackboard and chalk as well. Card games such as Snap and Go Fish can be easily taught to children of this age as well as board games such as Snakes and Ladders, and Memory. Dominoes is also popular.

A two-wheeler bike with trainer wheels and helmet is now appropriate as well as scooters or sleds, if you live near the snow!

Make a sewing card. Draw a picture on a piece of card (remember you do not need to be an artist and your child will still appreciate your pictures!). Make holes with a needle every 2 cm. The child can use a large needle and wool to 'sew' the card.

SCHOOL-AGE CHILDREN: FIVE TO SEVEN

A child of this age is seeking out new information, experiences and challenges in their play. School opens up a whole new world to them and they become more independent with their reading, writing and craft activities. They still value your input but may want you to spend a little more time on the sideline.

Children this age still love to pretend. They will set up their 'houses' and 'shops' and 'hospitals' and role play for hours. They will enjoy more complex construction sets and train sets with whole villages.

Active games are important as these children start to rely on friends a lot more. Ball games, bushwalking, swimming and whatever other sports your child or your family is interested in can be encouraged. An early introduction to sports and outdoor activities teaches your child about a healthy lifestyle which promotes exercise and good fun.

Science kits, craft kits, marbles and other hobby equipment will occupy them for hours. Some children will enjoy video and other electronic games. Board games are a great family activity, including chess, Monopoly and Scrabble.

Although your child may seem 'grown up' in lots of ways, children of this age often still enjoy the company of a favourite teddy or soft toy. It serves as a companion and protector during difficult times and should not be frowned upon. Sometimes we have seen our children express their feelings and concerns to a doll rather than to us. It may give them the confidence to express it to an adult at a later time.

THE ROLE OF MUSIC AND OTHER SOUNDS

Music and rhythm are part of our environment. You needn't have belonged to the school choir to enjoy bopping along to the Top 40. Your child won't mind if you sing out of tune, not until he gets older anyway, so long as you can share the pleasures of music with him. The listening skills children learn through musical activities can help their whole development. After all, just about every activity at school depends on listening. The creative side of music becomes a useful tool for expression and once again links the child with his environment.

Children learn to respond to music very early and soon begin to involve themselves, even before they are born. Many women experience their babies responding to music at some stage during pregnancy. One of our children was always soothed and comforted by a violin concerto but would give a violent kick to jazz!

This quietening and sudden reaction can also be observed in the very young baby. Soon he starts moving his body and swaying and later he copies rhythm and sounds. Initially you will provide the music and words and help your child do the actions. Then, after many repetitions, encourage your child to take an active part if he is not already doing so spontaneously. Body coordination and physical development will clearly benefit from musical activities.

Music activities for your child are easy to organise. All you need is the two of you and your voices. You can make music in the car, in the bath, in the park, anywhere! Music activities are great for your child's language development because they can include:

- vocal play;
- actions as well as talking;
- physical contact;
- repetition;
- turn-taking;
- nonverbal responses.

The listening skills children learn through musical activities can help their whole development. Children learn to respond to music very early. Music activities for your child are easy to organise. All you need is the two of you and your voices.

Rhyme and rhythm

One of the most important things children learn from musical and other sound activities is sound awareness. Your child may have perfect hearing but he needs to understand and respond to what he hears. Let him listen to all kinds of sounds: personal (sneezing), environmental (tap running), lullabies, marches, instrumental, orchestral. By doing this you are helping your child to respond appropriately to different sounds.

Every day we react to many sounds in our environment: the car screeching, sirens going, the school bell ringing in the morning. Attentive listening helps your child notice different speech sounds such as the quiet *t* sound, the louder *d* sound and the long *s* sound. The Sound Play box on pages 102–103 gives other suggestions for activities based on sound.

Listening also helps your child learn to associate words and actions. Nursery rhymes, action rhymes and finger games are useful for teaching your child to pay attention. If you exaggerate the rhyme and leave pauses, your child will learn to anticipate. In 'Humpty Dumpty', for example, you will find he is leaning over before you have even said the words 'had a great fall'.

As your child gets older you can replace the key word and make it more stimulating. Most two- to two-and-a-half-year-olds find it great fun if you sing 'Baa baa black cow'. See if he can spot the mistake?

Try to keep rhymes brief and interesting. Make the actions near your face to encourage the child to look at your lips, eyes and hands. Play finger games where you touch some part of his body. 'Incy wincy spider', 'This little piggy', and 'Open, shut them' are all good for this. Action songs are good for teaching turn-taking and imitation. Such songs include 'Ring-a-ring-a-roses', 'Row, row, row your boat', 'The wheels on the bus', and 'Johnny works with one hammer'.

Using rhymes is a very good way to extend memory and even aid learning. Rhyming and understanding the similarity of patterns is essential for early reading skills. With the Sesame Street 'Alphabet Song', your child will remember the tune and rhythm well before he learns the letters. (You'll remember from Chapter 2 that even when you are just talking, children will copy the rhythm of the talking first. A child who is used to hearing you say 'Where are you?' will often be able to say 'Air ar oo?' with the rise and fall of your voice copied perfectly long before he can pronounce the words correctly.)

Rhythm can also help children learn to spell, especially longer words. Most of us learned to count by using some rhythmical pattern, such as number tables.

Music can make daily routines and difficult times easier for your child and for yourself. For example, if he needs to walk some distance, make up a song about 'walking in the city'. You could do the same for activities such as washing his hair and sitting on the potty.

Rhythm instruments such as drums can be used to express feelings:

'How does this boy feel?'
'He's angry.'
'Let's play the drum in an angry way.'

Language concepts through music

Many language concepts can be taught through music. Your child can run fast or slow to the music. He can dance on tip-toe for high notes and on the ground for low notes. He might love to stamp his feet for loud sounds and creep for soft quiet sounds. Can he pick out long notes and short notes? Colours could also be taught by having instruments colour coded.

As your child gets older, music can be linked to stories and poetry. A story such as *The Three Bears* could be used. Make musical sounds for different parts of the story and include a variety of rhythm patterns and pitch and speech patterns. Other stories to try are *The Gingerbread Man, Puff the Magic Dragon, Rudolf the Red-Nosed Reindeer* and *The Three Billy Goats Gruff*. For more ideas, see the children's booklist at the back of this book.

Songs are often poems that have been set to tunes. Your child will enjoy making up his own tune for a verse. Once he is old enough to be more aware of speech sounds, experiment with both vowel and consonant sounds. Can he change the pitch and volume as he says 'm' and 'ah'?

One of the most important aspects of using music with your child is that it is enjoyable for both of you. You do not have to be a trained opera singer to sing and have fun with your child! Many children love using a tape-recorder and this is an ideal way to pass

SOUND PLAY

- Teach your child 'Old Macdonald had a farm'. You can have great fun pretending to be different animals and making their noises. You might also make a mobile of animals either drawn or cut from magazines. Your child will be able to discover the sound of paper crinkling and the sound of crayons on paper, too.

- Repeat patterns of claps using three to five beats of varying speed and volume.

- Ask your child to run around the garden, only stopping when you blow a whistle. How quickly can he respond?

- Use household items like pots, bowls and shoe boxes as drums. They will all give a different tone.

- Have your child choose which instrument is being played from items such as a bottle shaker and bell.

- Ask your child to decide whether you are clapping, knocking or beating. Is it loud or soft?

- Make different voices — happy, sad and loud ones, high-pitched and low-pitched ones.

- Draw teddies with different faces — sad, happy, surprised, tired. Ask your child to match the voice to the face.

- Find the hidden music box. Play the child's music box hidden under a blanket or furniture. See if he can find where the music is coming from.

- Dramatise a character or object such as a tree standing with its branches reaching high into the sky, or a snake slithering low on the ground.

- Use television programs like, *Playschool*, as sources of ideas for musical activities.

- Expose your child to different types of music — jazz, classical, pop and so on.

- Sing favourite nursery rhymes or songs. Perhaps change some of the words.

- Dance to music. Encourage different actions to match the changes in music, for example, scurry like mice, stand like giants, fly like aeroplanes.

- You and your child can clap to music, altering the speed and volume as appropriate.

- Make up songs to familiar melodies.

- Make up games with rhyming words. 'What do you hit a ball with that rhymes with (sounds like) cat?'

- Whisper speech sounds.

- Bang out names and messages, with one beat for each syllable — gar-den, An-na-bel.

- Play 'Musical bumps'. Your child jumps up and down to the music but must sit down quickly when the music stops.

the hours when driving long distances or flying. Remember not to exclude all conversation.

Remember too that children grow tired of, or outgrow songs so always keep a lookout for new ones. There are many cassettes and CDs available for young children including the *ABC for Kids* series with Peter Combe, and among the most popular, The Wiggles, Hi5 and S-Club 7.

Older children may like to use a walkman or discman sometimes, which means you can each listen to your own music or stories. There is now an enormous range of stories available on tape or CD for listeners of all ages. Check your toy library or local council library regularly for new releases. Listen to them with your child and have fun!

If your child shows interest and it is feasible, do allow him the experience of learning a musical instrument. Learning an instrument aids and strengthens auditory discrimination and memory. It also provides an outlet for expression of needs and feelings. There is also a substantial amount of research indicating that listening to certain types of classical music can aid feelings of wellbeing and academic performance. Already in the music shops there is a wide range of classical music for babies to listen to.

Music also plays an important role in influencing your child's moods and emotions. It can make him feel good, relaxed or provide the means of turning a negative mood into a more positive one.

THE ROLE OF TELEVISION

Both adults and children watch television for entertainment, education and information. Whatever the reason for television viewing, there are important advantages and disadvantages for your child.

Precisely because it is a tool for entertainment, education and information, television can play a constructive part in a child's life. The years of highest television viewing are often between the ages of two and four, coinciding with a critical time in the development of language, imagination and many other skills. Thus, a child who spends much of his day watching television is missing out on practising skills such as running, playing, looking at books and, very importantly, talking.

Carmen Luke, in her book *TV and Your Child*, says: 'Cumulative television hours — say, three to five hours of unmediated daily viewing — over the first four to five years in the child's life may impede the development of manual dexterity, as well as other social and verbal skills, at a crucial developmental stage.'

Television as teacher

Television is a powerful teacher, and what it teaches may be good or bad. Let's look first at the good side. Used wisely, television can certainly have many advantages. Substantial research shows that appropriate television viewing can enhance play and creativity. Many young children tend to play and watch television at the same time; television may stimulate play ideas and even pretend characters.

Television can also help increase your child's vocabulary and be the starting point for language-building activities. Your presence and

TELEVISION VIEWING

In 1990, the Australian Children's Television Foundation estimated that one million children watched approximately 23 hours of television every week, with preschoolers averaging 30 hours. This is more time for watching television than for any other activity except sleeping, and as much time as some students spend gaining a university degree.

participation gives your child greater opportunity to express thoughts and feelings. It can help your child retain information because you can sing along and repeat words later and even draw pictures, letters and numbers when the program is finished.

If you know what your child has watched, you can have him re-tell the program as a bedtime story or you can re-tell the story together and practise turn-taking skills. If you are actively participating in the viewing, you will know if your child uses what he has seen and heard constructively in other activities.

You can discuss the program contents as well as its positive and negative aspects during and after viewing. Home video-recorders allow you to record, review and discuss programs together. Studies show that by discussing a program with your child you can increase the benefits and reduce any negative effects. It gives you the opportunity to explain the meaning of new words and to clarify controversial scenes.

Television can help with the learning of language concepts, especially the more abstract concepts of time and space which you could discuss, for example, when Big Bird plays hide-and-seek in *Sesame Street*. It is the strong visual component which aids this learning. Watching a program with your child can set the scene for another hour of fun play afterwards. If they had been talking about position concepts during the program, you could then make an obstacle course with your child, relating it to the activities you have viewed.

Watching television can relax and soothe young children as well as excite and stimulate them. Most toddlers like to watch television for a

GUIDELINES FOR TELEVISION VIEWING

- Keep television viewing as a positive activity right from the beginning. Encourage particular programs and know what your child is watching.

- Help your child understand why he is watching television. This will encourage him to be active, and by using more cognitive effort he will learn to become more critical in viewing and thinking.

- If your baby or toddler watches television from a restricted place, such as a high chair, there is no alternative but to watch. If children are on the floor or in baby walkers they at least have the chance to move away when they want to. This will help them learn to watch and listen more selectively.

- Young children like having the volume switched up high but check it's not too loud. It can damage their hearing.

- Try to watch the television with your child if you can. This will make it easier to lead the conversation towards what the show is about: maybe an unusual character or specific words are used. Ask questions and encourage your child to make comments. Even with very young children, you can encourage and increase their attention span as well as help them to follow actions.

- Some parents report that television triggers 'bad' habits such as thumb-sucking. If such habits do occur, closer supervision is certainly required while the child is watching television.

- Television programs can interfere with family times. Mealtimes are one of the most important times for a child to practise his developing communication skills. Sitting at a table without the interruption of television is also desirable if the child is to learn the manual skills of eating and also table manners. He needs to watch the model of other family members and cannot do that if he is or they are watching television at the same time. Video-recorders can help here if you use them to tape a favourite program to watch at a more suitable time.

- Be careful of advertising which can indoctrinate very young children about junk foods, toys and behaviour.

short period each day and it can be a useful and pleasant pastime. After the child has been busily playing, he might enjoy just sitting and watching a suitable program.

Too much television

On the down side, as well as excluding the child from other activities, as already mentioned, too much television viewing can restrict the development of more complex language skills. Many programs contain sentences that are simple in form and therefore do not provide the opportunity to extend the child's existing language structures. Listen to the program and ask yourself: 'Is this how I want my child to talk?'

Television programs should be appropriate and match your child's level of understanding and life experiences. Television programs are graded in the following way so parents can assess whether they are suitable:

P Preschool children.

C Children 6–12 years of age.

G General exhibition.

PG Parental guidance recommended for children under 15 years of age.

M Recommended for mature audiences only.

MA Recommended for mature audiences over 15 years. These programs should not be screened before 9 p.m. and should carry a warning.

MAV Recommended for mature audiences over 15 years. These programs should not be shown earlier than 9.30 p.m. They include violence.

You should also be aware of commercials played during children's viewing times — they may cause more headaches than the program. The fast and often complex verbal messages used may not be understood by your child, which can lead to tears later. If all the child understood was that it was a 'big car' but not that it required batteries and a special track to operate on, he cannot understand why you won't buy it for him!

As well as exposure to what may be considered unrealistic values, exposure to violence is one of the most pervasive concerns about television watching for young children. Studies have indicated that by their mid-teens children will have seen tens of thousands of violent incidents and thousands of deaths. These will have been portrayed in both cartoon and realistic form and will have been screened in so-called 'children's viewing hours'. For children, indirect experiences seen on television can be just as powerful as real personal experiences. It has been proven that this violence is causing children to become less sensitive to the use of violence in real life, feeling concerned about the 'scary' world they appear to live in and being more likely to use aggression to solve conflict.

Television can become a part of the daily routine for many children from the age of three months. How many mothers do you know who turn on the television every day when they sit down to feed their baby? It doesn't take long for this to become a daily ritual.

Think about what your child might be doing if he wasn't glued to the screen. Is he missing out on learning other important skills? What about time for talking, reading, playing, walking and jumping?

Television should never be a substitute for reading. In fact there is no substitute for reading! Children who see their parents use television as the main means of entertainment, rather than reading, may not be as willing to look at books. Remember children's viewing habits tend to reflect those of their parents.

Your child would be far better off out in the fresh air on a summer's day getting exercise by running, jumping or playing with the dog than being cooped up in the air-conditioned family room watching cartoons! You are more likely to see your child with that spaced-out stare in front of the television than when he's racing his Matchbox cars up and down the pathway.

Playing and talking with you or a friend provide many more opportunities for active interaction than sitting in front of the television.

While television can help your child learn, it should never replace — can never replace — conversation or reading aloud as the best stimulation for language development.

What to watch

Are you panicking that your child watches too much television? Relax! We are not anti-television. We have all been guilty of using *Playschool* as a babysitter while we get on with other chores. We are just suggesting that television can play a more constructive part in your family life.

So, what should your child watch? It is wise to adopt the approach of moderate and balanced viewing of a variety of programs. Spend some time with your child watching programs and make a choice together.

What are our opinions on children's programs such as *Sesame Street* and *Playschool*? *Sesame Street* does create a fast pace with rapid jumps from one thing to another. In contrast, *Playschool* goes at a much slower pace in its actions and its speech. It tends to focus more on play and craft and does not rely on visual and auditory 'attention grabbers'. *Playschool* brings your child closer to what is going on and has a much more personal feel to it. Instructions are slow and clear and give your child time to act, if he chooses, on what he has just heard.

The *Book Place* is a popular program in South Australia for preschoolers and even older children. It is a local production and is highly interactive. Like *Playschool* it has a personal feel and the pace is quite steady — not too fast. Storytelling and singing are strong features and each show has one particular book which is recommended for the audience to read.

In choosing programs, try to aim for effective viewing that is only one part of daily family interaction, play and education. The guidelines will help you achieve this. Remember that you can restrict and negotiate which programs are seen, even with a three-year-old. This will encourage him to plan, to be selective and to savour his program rather than just watching an endless stream.

With your older child, it is just as important to monitor programs. Ideally a program will not only be entertaining but will also teach your child about the world around him. Try to negotiate a suitable limit for the amount of television allowed each day. The general consensus for children is no more than two hours of screen viewing per day and that includes computers!

THE ROLE OF COMPUTERS

According to the Australian Bureau of Statistics (May 2001) 53 per cent of households in Australia have at least one computer and one-third have Internet access. Families with dependent children are most likely to have a computer and Internet access, while single people are the least likely. The figures are similar in the UK and the USA.

As with television and videos/DVDs you may have some concern as to how much time your child should spend using the computer and indeed when they should start learning about this technology. The Australian Bureau of Statistics found that 95 per cent of children in Australia aged between five and 14 years have used a computer.

There are both advantages and disadvantages of using a computer but generally it is not the technology that causes a problem but the way in which it is put to use.

It may take your child some time to learn the basics of working the computer and coordination may play a role, especially in the use of the mouse. His fine-motor coordination will develop but if you wish, you can buy a special mouse or tracker ball, which moves more easily for younger children. Some activities use a touch-screen facility, which may be easier for the younger child. If your child has difficulty with the keyboard you can obtain a lowercase keyboard or an overlay board. Headphones can be used if the noise is distracting and will help your child stay focused on the activity.

The main danger with the computer is, like television, that your child will spend more time at the computer and less time in social activities with their peers. If possible, set up the computer in a place where an adult can be close by to help out if necessary. Just be careful that you aren't adding to the noise level in the room especially if the television is on at the same time.

Try and be aware of when and what your child is doing on the computer. With very young children you have greater control as they will need your help to access a program and you will be the one buying and loading the software he will be using.

Choosing software

Consider carefully the software you purchase: whether it is educational or just pure entertainment. Both can be worthwhile and both have a place. Don't fall into the trap of thinking that because software claims to be educational, it won't matter how long your child plays the program. As with any advertising, do check it matches up to its claims and is genuinely educational.

There is an increasing range of low-budget software and some games are even available free over the Internet. Monitor what you buy. As with movies, computer games are labelled with a classification on the package. Software programs vary enormously, some require right/wrong responses, while others require more involved participation. Both types have a place, depending on the aim of the activity.

For the computer to be useful, your child needs to be able to use it without too much fuss and effort and the software must be practical. Apart from checking whether the program is attractive to your child with its use of pictures, colours and activities, check also whether it is user-friendly.

CHECKLIST FOR ACQUIRING USER-FRIENDLY SOFTWARE

- Does your child always have to start at the beginning of the program or can he go straight to the point where he previously left off?

- How easily can you change the activities?

- Are the keys simple and easy to use?

- If there is speech used, how easy is it to understand the accent or computerised tone?

- Do the activities change quickly or do they take a long time to load?

- Is the program too busy or the background music too distracting?

- Are the instructions clear and simple?

- Does the program target specific skills?

If you can, try and experiment with the software before you buy it. The blurb on the back may sound interesting but you won't know until you see the program in action. Decide what you are looking for in the software and then see if it meets that aim. If it is educational, is it based on developmental levels and sound teaching practices? Is it slow and boring or is it interactive and providing immediate feedback? Does it have any cultural bias?

Before you buy a program, check that the program is relatively straightforward to install and run. Also remember to check that the program's computer requirements match the facilities your computer can offer. There is nothing more frustrating than viewing an excellent product at the shop, only to find when you load it on to your own computer that you do not have the appropriate sound or video cards etc. Either you have the expense of upgrading your computer or a program that won't work properly.

Software programs for language activities are improving but still can't replace interaction with other people. Although some programs target specific aspects of communication very effectively and successfully, it is probably best to view the computer as an additional tool in helping development and not as a substitute for your own time and input. However, we know from our own experience with expatriate families in Indonesia that the computer and the Internet can provide a lifeline. Not only does the Internet allow them to keep in touch with their families, news and culture back home, it can also be an enormous source of support with programs and information for children with special needs. Whether you live overseas or in remote parts of your own country it can often be difficult to access professional services. Email will enable you to keep in regular contact with the appropriate professional who can guide you through a program. Some excellent programs such as Fast ForWord (Scilearn) can be carried out through the Internet.

There are a number of stimulating computer games available through which your child can develop and play the activities at his own pace. These are enjoyable because he can play a game repetitively without anyone getting bored or frustrated, as can happen with friends or family;

the *immediate* feedback is much more fun and it allows your child to have many attempts; and if he does something wrong the computer is very patient and will often help him through to a correct response.

It is easy for children or adults to become addicted to exciting, fast-moving computer or video games. Children these days can even watch a movie on their computer. Some research has shown that excessive use can lead to poor social and communication skills, inadequate eating and sleeping habits, problems with schoolwork and a poor attention span in the classroom. It is difficult for a teacher to compete with the whiz-bang action on a computer. Keep your eyes open for any sign of addictive behaviour especially if your child is cutting back on the amount of time spent with friends or other activities. A few children can be so obsessed that their only topic of conversation is computer games.

Using the Internet

The National Schools Board Foundation (USA) research found that use of the Internet provides a positive force in children's education. Over 40 per cent of children aged between nine and 17 years said that the Internet has improved their attitude to attending school. Parents also reported that using the Internet had not significantly changed their children's participation in other activities. Almost all parents participating in the survey felt their children spent the same amount of time reading, playing outdoors and spending time with their families. However, 37 per cent of parents felt that their children have watched less television since they were introduced to the Internet. Parents continued to express their concern about unsupervised Internet access.

The Internet is a fantastic tool. It can provide both you and your child with opportunities to get information, play games, communicate with others and even go shopping. However, there are no rules and regulations covering the content of what is placed on the Internet and we're sure there are many activities that you would not like your child to be involved in. It is possible to access sites not related to the topic you are looking for. There is however, software you can buy or even download from the Internet, which screens and filters the content that your child has access to. One popular website providing this 'net nanny' is www.crayoncrawler.com.

Ways of filtering information on the Internet are developing all the time and further information is available on Young Media Australia's website www.youngmedia.org.au. Some service providers have safety nets for child users so discuss using them. Try and teach your child to be selective and explain why selectivity is important. If you make sensible rules for use of the computer and Internet, you will reduce the risks of any problems arising and increase the benefits that using this technology can offer. Encourage your child to discuss with you any queries they might have or any experiences that seem unusual.

Do be aware that not all the information on the Internet is accurate. Information can come from many different sources and anyone can set up a web site and place information on it. It is also possible to come across unpleasant material unexpectedly while you are searching for a site or someone can send inappropriate messages.

It is beneficial if you can be comfortable enough with technology so at least you know the basics of finding your way around. Do try and keep track of the web sites that your child is visiting. You can obtain this information by looking in 'History', 'Options' or 'Preferences' menus, which will tell you which sites were visited most recently.

Make sure that your child knows NEVER to give out his name or contact details including email address. They should not be tempted to fill out questionnaires. If the activity asks for these details your child needs to know that they do not have to do everything the computer says and this information must not be given. If in doubt they should ask your advice. Make sure you are aware if your child is using email or chat lines and supervise this closely.

If you feel that your child has become 'hooked' and is using the Internet so excessively that they have become withdrawn do seek advice. Otherwise careful monitoring and encouraging your child to view games and information critically and selectively should overcome any potential problems. The Australian Broadcasting Authority's website www.aba.gov.au/family/index/html is designed to help families get the best out of the Internet while protecting children from the worst.

Another useful parents' guide to the Internet is the website: www.parentsoup.com/onlineguide/.

Of course the Internet provides an enormous resource to you as a parent not just for activities for your child but on parenting skills and on information about development and difficulties. Remember that, as indicated earlier, not all information is accurate but it does provide an excellent starting point. See 'Useful websites for parents and children' at the back of this book.

7 **The role of books**

Why should we write about books for preschool children? How will this help your child to talk? Quite simply, books provide almost unlimited possibilities for learning not only about the world but also about how to use language. Reading itself is not a 'natural' process. Reading and writing skills need to be taught in much the same way as learning to play the piano. Research demonstrates that we all use the same skills in order to make sense of the written word. However, not everyone learns these skills in the same way, in the same order, at the same speed or even at the same age. Many children make smooth steady progress throughout the different reading stages, seemingly without much effort, others take longer to start or to progress. Whichever learning process your child is using, you can still help at home. You are probably already helping reading skills without even knowing it; maybe you have shown your child how his name looks written down or what street signs mean. These are important steps to understanding the meaning and value of the printed word.

The first steps to reading

Reading books together is an excellent activity which stimulates your child's talking and provides a foundation of pre-reading skills.

A child can enjoy and benefit from being read to right from birth. Keep a selection of books within easy reach and make a practice of showing them to him early, even from the day you first bring him home. Why not snuggle up on the sofa with your newborn and share the delights of your magazine? It doesn't have to be a baby book. Your baby will enjoy the physical contact and listening to your voice as you read to him.

It is also good to have some special baby books. Uncluttered books with bright primary colours are often more attractive to your child than the books illustrated in subtle colours which seem to be more attractive to adults.

Your baby will probably want to grab the book — this is his way of telling you he is interested. You'll be astonished at how early he may give signs of knowing which book he is looking at.

As your baby becomes more mobile, he will want to be physically active even when reading. Use rhythm and actions — when reading 'Humpty Dumpty', pretend to fall with your child at the appropriate time. Tickle or cuddle at a particular point and you'll find that your baby begins to anticipate it, if you give him time. Even by six months he may become excited when he recognises a picture of a familiar person or toy.

Wordless picture books can open doors to your baby's imagination. Books by Dick Bruna and the *First Picture Books* in the Ladybird series are good examples. There is a wide range of books on the market suitable for babies. Rag and boardbooks are a matter of taste — be guided by your child as some children just don't respond to them. There are also many bath books available. Many children enjoy homemade scrapbooks or photographs of themselves and their family, so keep a book of old Christmas and birthday cards handy for these times.

Remember that if you decide to use ordinary paper books with your very young child, they will not be kept in pristine condition. If you are concerned about the condition books are kept in, perhaps keep some special ones aside for later. At this young age we don't want the child to learn that an adult becomes angry when he touches a book. Our

BOOKS AND YOUR BABY

- Learning to read will be easier if your child is used to looking at books.

- Books are a good source of topics to talk about.

- Reading to your baby encourages him to listen.

- Start with simple, brightly coloured books.

- Make looking at books a regular part of each day.

- Point out to your child that there are other things to read beside books.

- Use the library.

---

view is if the child has learnt from the book, does it matter if it is dog-eared and has pages repaired with sticky tape? There is time for learning how to look after books later, when they have the manual dexterity to be more careful.

Books of nursery rhymes are good to introduce at any time. They are popular with even the youngest children because of their catchy phrasing. Intonation and rhythm become more meaningful, and through having nursery rhymes read over and over the child will eventually recognise the words. Memorising plays an important part in early reading. All children, for the same reasons, love tickling games and finger play with repetitive lines. Nursery rhymes seem to have lost popularity in recent years but because we now know the range of skills that these rhymes teach for early reading, we would like to see them make a big comeback. So do your child a favour and teach him some nursery rhymes.

As your baby grows, try to find the time to read to him, a little at a time and frequently. Choose a peaceful time when neither of you is too tired. Let your baby see the book and give him time to look at the pictures and respond. It will be more fun if you choose books that you and your child can both enjoy.

As he gets older, constant repetition of favourite stories will give your child an intuitive feeling about the patterns and structures of language. By the time he is 18 months old, *you* may be bored by the constant repetition of the same story but he will be delighted. He will also love stories with repetitive lines, like 'Who sank the boat?' each time you turn the page. Reading aloud is an excellent turn-taking activity — if you pause, your child can fill in the words.

One of the aims of reading to your child is to provide language that he can imitate at some later time. It will also stimulate him to both give and receive some simple information about the book you're looking at. Your child's contribution will depend on his level of language development. Your response can provide him with a model or prompt for a greater contribution. For example, if he just says 'Thomas', you might say:

'Look at naughty Thomas! What's going to happen?'

Welcome any observation about the pictures.

As your child gets older he will prefer a simple story. Three-year-olds like books that tell a story and have an ending that makes sense. Books can be used to help your young child understand and cope with new situations and feelings such as going to hospital or the arrival of a new baby. *Za-Za's Baby Brother* is a wonderful storybook to have if there is a new baby coming into your home.

Don't feel that you have to buy books. Books about your family can be of more interest. Making a book is one of the simplest ways of encouraging a child to become a storyteller. The child creates his own original works featuring himself and other close people. With help a child of three can make 'What I did today' books. His little sentences become books once you write them down; the children draw pictures or you use photographs and then give the pages a cover. Easy access to crayons will encourage your child to scribble, draw and write. This is a great way to increase a child's confidence.

Continuing to use conversational strategies with children of four years of age and older will stimulate their language and thinking skills. Try to use what you have been reading about as a starting point for discussing the child's own past or anticipated experiences and feelings:

if reading *Thomas the Tank Engine,* you might remind him of his visit to the train museum or trains that you have seen. Do real trains look the same?

Reading to your child does not have to be limited to books. Encourage an interest in everything from labels to signs, brochures, menus, and words that flash up in television commercials. A child learns early that print representations stand for objects. In fact they learn this before you expect them to. For example, young children know that yellow arches signify McDonald's and STOP on a hexagonal red and white sign means you don't go on.

Read-and-talk time

Books are a perfect example of how learning to talk ties in with talking to learn. Whether you are reading aloud to your child or whether he is just looking at the pictures, talking should be part of the activity. Some writers refer to this as 'read-and-talk time'. You can talk before reading, during reading and after reading.

As soon as you show your child the cover of the book and tell him the title, his imagination will start to work. Set the scene by giving a one-sentence summary of the story and perhaps asking a key question.

A favourite story of ours is *My Hippopotamus Is On Our Caravan Roof Getting Sunburnt* by Hazel Edwards. When reading this book, you might say:

> *'This is about a hippopotamus who goes to the beach for a holiday with the little girl's family.'*

Then you could add:

> *'You've been to the beach. Did we take a hippopotamus on our holiday?'*

Any child we've read this book to is already bursting with questions before we've even started reading. You can answer some questions, but then suggest:

> *'Let's read the story to see what happens.'*

When children look at a book such as *My Hippopotamus* ... the first thing that grabs their attention is the pictures: 'Wow! Look at that hippo eating cake!'

We have shared this book with the same children many times and on occasions don't read any of the text. The pictures are enough to spark off a story and conversation between the reader and the child.

Whether your four-year-old wants you to read or your two-year-old just wants to look at and talk about the pictures, you can still stir up the imagination. Ask questions like:

> *'What will happen if the hippo doesn't put his floatie on?'*
> *'Why is the hippo wearing sunglasses?'*

Ask your child if he knows anyone who wears sunglasses.

Stories are also a good way to talk about your child's feelings. Help him to relate the feelings of the characters to his own everyday experiences:

> *'How did you feel when you caught a fish with Daddy*
> *at the beach?'*
> *'Do the mum and dad look tired?'*
> *'What does Daddy like to do when he's tired?'*

Explain causes and effects and see if your child can guess what might happen on the next page:

> *'Will the hippo go shell hunting?'*

There are endless dialogues that can go on between you and your child when reading a book together. It is these dialogues which will stimulate your child's language and stretch his thinking.

When are children ready to learn to read?

Traditionally children begin to learn to read on starting school. Many children, in fact, are ready before this time. However, there's no need to teach your preschool child to read in a formal way. As with talking, your child will learn a great deal about reading from watching you.

BOOKS AND YOUR PRESCHOOL CHILD

- Books help develop a child's concentration and attention span.

- Parents' natural responses (imitating, labelling, expanding, promoting and repetition) are all part of sharing a book and developing language.

- Books help develop a vocabulary and verbal skills.

- Parents can initiate specific learning by choosing specific books.

- Books help develop thinking and imagination.

- Children will enjoy the stories and want to learn to read.

- Books help to develop awareness of specific concepts related to reading, for instance following the text from left to right, and from top to bottom.

- It can be very useful to take a book for your child while you are:
  – in a waiting room,
  – on a bus or train,
  – having a lunch break when shopping,
  – waiting in a shop.

As we have already discussed, one of the major ways children learn is through imitation. They not only imitate sounds but also the actions of adults and older children, so if they see people around them reading and experiencing books, they will follow that example. By watching you, your child will learn how books work; that is, you start at the beginning and turn the pages over to work your way to the back of the book. As he watches you run your finger under the text, he will realise that the words on the page have meaning and that we work through the sequence from left to right.

Keep your child's books within easy reach and he will eventually sort through them and 'read' them alone, or initiate the activity by bringing the book to you.

As your child gets older, choose books you both enjoy. If you find the story boring, it is difficult to read it with enthusiasm, and enthusiasm is important in encouraging him to eventually enjoy reading himself. There will be times when your child will want the same book over and over again. Perhaps this is a good time to take turns — your child chooses one book, you choose the next.

Early beginner books stress word recognition through repetition. Reading is not a matter of recognising words first and then getting the meaning, but rather the meaning guides and aids the recognition of words.

Books are not the only tools to use in helping your child learn to read. Although learning to read can be quite repetitious, there are all sorts of games which can take the boredom out of the repetition, and some of these are described below. The first step is often to build up a vocabulary of familiar names and labels that your child recognises by sight.

It is preferable to use lowercase letters when writing, not capital letters. Make use of phonics, where we use the letter's sound rather than its name: 'a' as in 'apple'. The Sounds of Letters on page 130 gives a full alphabet of phonics.

FAMILY NAMES

Make name cards for each member of the family, including visitors such as grandparents and pets.

A Before a meal, place each card at the appropriate place at the dinner table.

B Draw family members and find the appropriate name cards to go with the drawings.

C Muddle all the cards together. Work out what each card says and give it to the person. Perhaps stick it to their foreheads? They look very silly and that's part of the fun.

D Musical hats — pin a name card to a hat. Pass around the hat when the music is playing. When the music stops, the person holding the hat has to read the card and place it on the appropriate person's head.

LABELS

Make two sets of cards for different items in the room. First, stick the labels on each item, then give the matching card to your child and see if he can find it.

After a while, take the labels down. Muddle them up and help your child read them and stick them back in the appropriate places. If he gets it wrong, make a joke of it:

'O-oh! He's put the word 'bed' on the door.'

Lean against the door and pretend to go to sleep. Have fun!

It's a good idea to make a habit of labelling windows, doors, cupboards and favourite toys around the house. Simply print the word on a piece of card and attach it to the object. Leave notes in lunch boxes and around the house. Use a wide vocabulary: children learn the shapes as well as the sounds of words. It also encourages guessing in context which is a valuable reading skill.

Another idea is to point out words when you are out shopping, such as 'Push' and 'Pull' on the doors; when your child draws a picture, write a couple of words on it to describe what is happening.

POST BOXES

Make two boxes with slits to post 'letters'. Write a letter onto two cards and stick one onto each box. On some old envelopes, write some simple words which begin with the same letters as on the boxes. Give one box to teddy and the other to rabbit. Pretend to be a postman with a bag full of letters. Check each envelope to see if the first letter is the same as on the box. If it is, post it.

PHRASES AND SENTENCES

Write down some action words on cards, such as 'hopping', 'tickling' and 'jumping'. Read them together and carry out the activity. This can be taken one step further by using the name cards as well to make phrases like 'Mummy jumping'. Children love seeing their parents make fools of themselves! As your child becomes familiar with individual words, you can start putting more of them together. Use your cards to make simple, fun sentences like 'Mummy is tickling Sarah', then carry out the action.

A FEW OTHER IDEAS

Sound scrap book When learning a new sound, write it in a scrapbook. Cut out pictures of objects starting with the sound and paste them into the book. Your child will love this activity, especially if you are not too fussy about neatness!

Sound skittles Use empty plastic bottles or skittles. Put a different letter on each skittle. Take turns in throwing the ball. Name the sound of the letter knocked over and ask:

'Can you think of a word beginning with that sound?'

I Spy An old favourite! 'I spy with my little eye something beginning with'... Choose the sound and ask others to guess what you can see.

How children learn to read

Your preschooler can now identify a few single words, which is great, but maybe he hasn't yet learnt to 'read' in the sense that we know it. That is, he can't yet tackle words that he has never seen before. Readers of all ages use a range of strategies when confronted with new or difficult words. These include:

* using clues from the pictures or the rest of the text;
* comprehension;
* using sight-recognisable vocabulary;
* using the initial letter as a clue;
* breaking words into segments;
* sounding out words;
* using sound rules;
* recognising patterns.

When your child starts school he will learn these skills, although their foundation is established with pre-reading activities and your child's understanding of rhythm and rhyme.

Some parents feel frustrated when teachers encourage their children to get clues from the pictures in a book. That's not really reading, is it? But it is a useful starting point and it is a cue that we use as adults if we get really stuck.

Another useful start to reading is to build a solid sight-vocabulary of frequently used words. This gives the child confidence and means that he doesn't have to struggle over every single word he comes across. Also, frequently used words, such as 'the' and 'are', are often words that just don't fit any pattern. They are words that have evolved over time and their pronunciation doesn't match the configuration of letters. However, we can't learn all words using our visual memory, as we simply cannot remember all words that exist by their visual pattern alone. Children need more strategies in order to develop fast and efficient word recognition. But building this core vocabulary of sight words does provide a strong beginning.

Once a strong foundation for reading is established, more specific strategies such as those described above are required to develop your child's reading skills. Although we all use a combination of the above strategies, research has shown that competent readers do not use contextual clues nearly as often as poor readers because they are able to decode the information much more rapidly. There are a group of skills that are now known to be essential for a child to become a competent reader. These skills are called 'phonological awareness'. Teachers, tutors and speech and language pathologists have been familiar with this term for many years. No matter which general approach to developing reading you believe in, research has shown that these skills are crucial. Many children pick them up developmentally, others work out these skills for themselves as they are taught to read. Reading activities for the first three years of school assume that the child is spontaneously developing these skills and the classroom teaching is built around this assumption. Reading difficulties are often not identified until a child reaches eight years of age when it is discovered they are unable to apply these strategies.

Phonological awareness skills have also been shown to be a powerful predictor of future reading achievement, including word recognition, reading comprehension and spelling skills. There is a considerable body of evidence that children who perform well on phonological awareness tests before they go to school will go on to be good readers. There is a direct correlation with phonological awareness skills at age four and reading ability at age eight. The good news is that these phonological awareness skills can be taught. A considerable body of research shows that children who are taught these phonological awareness skills achieve greater gains in their reading ability than children who are not.

WHAT IS PHONOLOGICAL AWARENESS?

Phonological awareness, or 'sound awareness', is the ability to perceive individual sounds within spoken words. It includes the development of the ability to recognise that a constant stream of speech when talking can be segmented into units from syllables to individual sounds.

The acquisition of these skills usually starts between the ages of four and seven. Your preschool child has very little awareness of sound and is very focused on meaning. Children in preschool do not necessarily know that speech can be broken up into segments or individual sounds. However, most children do bring into their first years at school their ability to 'play' with sounds, for example by rhyming words. This is extremely important. They may comment that a word sounds funny, or that it starts with the same sound as another, or sounds like another word. This often revolves around the accompanying toilet humour of the four-year-old, which irritates parents but sends their peers into stitches of laughter. These are the first steps in realising that a stream of speech can be broken down into units. Once they get to school they are taught that these individual sounds are represented in the alphabet as letters. It includes the knowledge that these individual sounds actually have a sequential pattern according to the rules of our language.

The range of phonological awareness skills are explained in the list on page 128. These may sound very complicated and perhaps you feel that some of these skills are unnecessary. But how many parents have assumed that because their child can spell the word 'cat' they must be

PHONOLOGICAL AWARENESS SKILLS

- Word awareness: where does one word end and the next one begin?

- Recognition and production of syllables: what is a syllable?

- Recognition and production of sounds.

- Recognition and production of rhyme: awareness of rhyming pattern and similar visual/auditory patterns.

- Recognition of sounds within words: initial, medial and final word-positions.

- Ability to isolate sounds in the initial, middle and final word-positions: where does one sound end and another one start?

- Isolating and producing sounds in the correct word order: the order of sounds most certainly makes a difference to meaning.

- Counting sounds: how many sounds can you hear in a word?

- Blending: recognising the word formed by a sequence of sounds.

- Deleting and adding sounds.

- Substituting a sound in a word after the sound is identified and new sounds supplied.

---

able to spell the words 'hat' or 'fat' or why not even 'cap'? To do this we are actually asking our children to apply these skills. What we are asking is:

- Can you hear that the word 'cat' is made up of three sounds: 'c-a-t'?
- Can you hear that 'fat' sounds like 'cat'?
- What part of the words sound the same? The beginning, the end or the middle?
- Can you take off that first sound and make our new word 'at'?

- Can you hear which sound the new word starts with, 'f'?
- Can you add that new sound on to the ending of the first word, 'f' plus 'at'?
- Do you know that the words look similar when written down? fat cat
- It all sounds so much more complicated now doesn't it?

When classroom teachers teach word groups such as 'at' or 'et' words, they are assuming that the children in their class can hear the sound patterns, see the visual similarities and carry out the tasks above. Not all children make this connection spontaneously and just tackle words as a group without appreciating the patterns and skills they are being shown. This is how problems can be missed until the later years.

SOUNDS

All that early play on words, rhythm and rhyme is extremely important for phonological awareness. To be able to play around with sounds your child really needs to know the phonic sounds of each letter. Understanding the alphabet is one of the most important skills your child will learn. Your child has to recognise the visual differences between each of the individual letters. They need to know the letters can be written in lower case and upper case (capital) form. They need to know each letter has a name, as when singing the alphabet, but that it also makes a sound. Your child needs to hear the difference between all the individual sounds and match them to the letter shape. It is these sounds that will get him started in reading and writing until he learns some rules and patterns of the written language. Not all parents are familiar with the sound each letter produces (phonics), so a list is provided on page 130.

Sometimes it helps to know the sound by hearing the consonant in the final-word position. In this way you can hear that 't' is *t* as in 'cat' not *ta* as in 'cata'.

The best way to start drawing attention to sounds is by using names — especially their own, for example, 'Ssssarah'. If you have chosen a name that doesn't match phonetically, for example, 'Charlotte' then you might want to start with 'Mum' or 'Dad'. You can purchase sets

THE SOUNDS OF LETTERS

a	apple	h	hand	o	orange	v	violin
b	bed	i	inside	p	pig	w	window
c	cat	j	jug	q	queen	x	axe
d	dog	k	key	r	rabbit	y	yawn
e	egg	l	leaf	s	sun	z	zip
f	fish	m	moon	t	tap		
g	gate	n	nose	u	up		

As you say the word pause after the first sound. This is the correct sound of the letter.

of uppercase and lowercase letters at most toyshops but it is very easy to make your own.

Later on your child will recognise blends (where letters go together) for example, *bl* as in 'blue', and diagraphs (where two letters make one sound) for example, *sh* as in 'ship'.

Developing reading skills

When your child first goes to school he will start bringing home a range of books to 'read', some may be picture books and others may be so beyond his reading ability that you read the book. But listen to what your child wants to say about the book. Don't you do all the talking!

Before you start to read, look at the front cover and help your child get as much information as he can about what might happen in the story. Look at the title and illustrations. Most early readers use a repetitive line and simple words. If your child does get stuck on a tricky word, try and work it out together:

'Can you guess what the word might be from the story?'
'What would make sense?'
'What sound does it start with?'
'Look at the picture, are there any clues?'

Don't interrupt the flow of reading for too long otherwise your child will get bored or even forget the context of the story. If your child cannot guess, tell him the word.

SIGHT WORDS FOR EARLY READING

a	he	I	of	that	was
and		in		the	
		is		to	
		it			

all	be	had	not	said	we
are	but	have		so	with
as		him	on		
at	for	his	one	they	you

about	did	if	no	right	want
an	do	into	new		well
	down		now	see	went
back		just		some	were
been	first				what
before	from	like	off	their	when
big		little	old	them	where
by	get	look	only	then	which
	go		or	there	who
came		made	other	this	will
call	he	make	out	two	
can	has	me	our		
come	him	more	over	up	your
could	here	much			
		must			

These three lists combined make up one-half of all children's reading material.

Source: E. W. Dolch, 220 world list (1947)

Your child's teacher will probably be building a vocabulary that can be recognised by sight. Learning these words will help the fluency of reading and keep reading moving along. The first words in his sight vocabulary might be his own name and place names. Your child will need to see these words frequently before he remembers them. If you are helping your child learn sight words please make it a game and not a chore. See Sight Words For Reading on page 131. These words occur frequently in written and spoken English.

You can write the words on cards and play games such as Lotto, Snap or Pairs. Point out these words when you see them in street signs or in magazines or newspapers.

We strongly recommend you avoid the temptation of testing your child. That kind of pressure is not necessary from family members. Because they are frequently occurring words, you will be able to tell if your child recognises them or not.

As your child moves on to longer books he may find the level of difficulty is not the problem, he may just get tired or the story is too slow for him. You can still help in several ways: you could take over the reading to move the story along; you could read one of the characters; or you could even try reading alternate pages.

When you notice your child is becoming a competent reader when reading out aloud, you could start encouraging him to read quietly to himself. But don't stop reading to him yourself at this stage. You can still read exciting novels that are too hard for him to tackle by himself.

Discussing a book is still extremely important. Encourage your child to actively think about the story by asking questions:

'What do you think might happen next?'
'Has that ever happened to you?'
'How do you think he feels?'
'Would you have done that?'
'What was your favourite part of the story?'

Asking questions and discussing the book is a great way to show you are interested in your child's views and ideas as well as building a strong foundation for learning.

Most children commence school with some general idea of what reading and writing is all about. During their first year at school this will be consolidated and strong foundations will be laid for literacy. As we have pointed out throughout this book children develop at different rates but there is a range of skills that are expected to develop during this first year. (See Literacy Skills Developed During the First Year at School on page 134 for reference.)

HOW YOU CAN HELP AT HOME

Your role as parents is extremely important in helping your child to develop his reading skills. A small amount of time each day playing sound or rhyme games, or reading or learning the alphabet all help to provide a strong foundation. Refer to the activities mentioned in 'The role of music and other sounds' and make sure your child has developed these foundation skills. Make reading an enjoyable part of your daily routine. Try and read the book with enthusiasm and talk about the story together; it can be very boring listening to a voice that lacks expression. Choose a book you enjoy too so that your interest comes through in your voice when you are reading. Aim for a steady speed as one of the hardest things to do when reading aloud is not to go too fast. You need to read slowly enough for your child to build up a picture of the story and digest all the information.

Bookshops usually stock the latest good quality books your child might enjoy. Libraries are also invaluable; it would be very expensive to purchase every book you read so take advantage of this wonderful resource.

When reading, try and sit side by side in a comfortable chair. Make sure the lighting is good and noise is kept to a minimum. Don't make your child choose between reading and watching the television or other activities. You know which one would win! All activities have a place so choose reading time carefully.

Some children, however, are so active you might wonder how you are going to get them to sit down for ten minutes. Try allowing them to draw or colour while you are reading so their hands are kept busy.

Learning to read must be a pleasurable, successful experience; we all

LITERACY SKILLS DEVELOPED DURING
THE FIRST YEAR AT SCHOOL

Your child will learn:

- which is the front of the book and which way the book opens
- the book tells a story
- the print goes from left to right
- the print tells the story
- the print starts at the top of the page
- the sequence goes from the left page then to the right page
- you must turn over the page to continue the story
- the story has a beginning, a middle and an end
- the writing is made up of words
- words are made up of letters
- a word on the page corresponds to a speech word
- there are spaces between words
- how to recognise letters — both upper case and lower case
- how to match a sound to a letter
- that pictures in the book relate to the story
- which words rhyme
- which words begin with the same sound
- which words end with the same sound
- to listen and understand stories read to them
- to respond to questions about the story they have heard
- to re-tell a story
- to recognise their name
- to recognise an increasing number of frequently used words
- to write across the page from left to right
- to write from top to bottom of the page
- to write their name
- to write letters of the alphabet
- to write an increasing number of words spelt correctly or in a decipherable way
- to write information/stories/ideas in a sentence form
- to understand and follow oral instructions
- to express ideas verbally.

know how frustrating learning a new task can be when someone is nagging and criticising our every step. Help your child to understand how useful reading is in everyday life. Point out notes you have received or written or signs and notices in the street.

English is a difficult language. If you read the following poem by T.S. Watt you will wonder how any of us learn to read at all!

Brush up your English

I take it you already know

Of tough and bough and cough and dough?

Others may stumble, but not you,

On hiccough, thorough, laugh and through.

Well done! And now you wish perhaps

To learn of less familiar traps?

Beware of heard, a dreadful word,

That looks like beard and sounds like bird.

And dead: it's said like bed not bead —

For goodness sake don't call it 'deed'.

Watch out for meat and great and threat

(They rhyme with suite and straight and debt.)

A moth is not a moth in mother

Nor both in bother, broth in brother.

And here is not a match for there,

Nor dear and fear for bear and pear.

And then there's dose and rose and lose —

Just look them up — and goose and choose,

And core and work, and card and ward,

And font and front and word and sword.

And do and go and thwart and cart —

Come, come, I've hardly made a start!

A dreadful language? Man alive,

I'd mastered it when I was five.

(T.S. Watt 1954)

'Brush Up Your English' by T.S Watt was reproduced from Yule, George, *Study of Language*, p.40, Cambridge University Press, UK. Reproduced with the permission of Cambridge University Press.

When your child starts reading he will stumble and make many mistakes. Don't worry, be positive and keep the activity moving along steadily.

Talk to your child's teacher about any concerns and support any work carried out in class. If you have further or specific concerns seek guidance from a speech pathologist or centre for children with specific learning difficulties. Don't be concerned about visiting a centre for children with reading difficulties even when your child is very young. You will find staff only too willing to guide you with early intervention/prevention support and advice.

If your child does experience difficulty don't stop reading to him. He is still able to enjoy listening to stories. Perhaps use taped stories as the music and different voices can add an element of fun. Try to choose books that will really capture his interest so that he wants to know what is going to happen next. Don't make the reading sessions too long or he will get tired and bored.

It is important that early reading experiences are positive. Your child will only want to learn to read if he finds stories fun and interesting and if he has success in the early stages. The children's booklist at the back of this book gives plenty of suggestions for children of all ages.

There are also some excellent Internet sites for early reading development as well as some excellent software. See 'Useful websites for parents and children' at the back of this book.

HOW TO IDENTIFY READING PROBLEMS

Sometimes it is difficult to know whether children have specific difficulties or whether they are just late developers. The phonological awareness skills discussed earlier are useful for all readers. At any level, the stronger these skills are then the stronger his reading skills will be. Helping to develop these skills can only aid your child's progress. For many children, intensive work on boosting these skills is enough. There are others, however, who have quite specific difficulties, often over and above their sound skills. These problems are known as 'specific learning difficulty' or 'dyslexia'.

IS YOUR CHILD AT RISK FOR LEARNING DIFFICULTIES

Family history Does any member of the extended family have speech, language or learning difficulties?

Delay in developmental speech milestones Is he progressing at a slower rate than his peers?

Poor phonological awareness skills Does he understand rhyme and identify auditory and visual patterns?

Word retrieval/word-finding problems Does your child have trouble recalling the names of people, places or things?

Poor on rapid naming tasks Does your child have difficulty naming items very quickly?

Poor verbal short-term memory Does he have trouble following lengthy instructions?

Find it difficult producing complex sound sequences in multisyllabic words (e.g. elephant, caterpillar, hospital) All children mispronounce some long words at some stage in their life, but have you noticed that many long words seem to be difficult?

Visual perceptual disorders Does your child have trouble understanding and remembering visually presented material?

A specific learning difficulty is the condition where a child experiences difficulty in learning to read and write. In practice it can be more complex than this. Specific learning difficulty can show itself in many different ways, but is usually identified when a child's reading is slow to develop. There are many different types of learning problems that interfere with the process of learning to read and write.

There is still considerable disagreement regarding the definition of dyslexia. Most teachers and speech pathologists use a child's general ability as a guideline: that a child of average general ability should be reading at an average level.

Specific learning difficulties can be associated with any other disorder, including clumsiness and slow general development.

There are clearly defined areas of development, detailed on page 137, that we know put children at risk for reading difficulties.

There are many books produced for parents and teachers on this subject. Refer to the lists of references and websites at the back of this book or contact your nearest professional centre.

8 Learning to talk in special situations

GROWING UP WITH MORE THAN ONE LANGUAGE

Millions of children around the world are exposed to two or sometimes more languages. This might be because the parents speak more than one language or because a child moves to live in another country. It can also be the result of the general increased interest in foreign languages, which has meant that many young children are placed in various forms of foreign language learning environments.

Research to date has not consistently shown bilingualism to have either positive or negative effects on a child's development. However, it is common for bilingualism to bring many advantages to a person, both as a youngster and later as an adult. Your child is very lucky if he can speak more than one language, because many extra opportunities will be open to him. He could more easily live and work in another country.

FEATURES OF BILINGUAL DEVELOPMENT

■ There is usually an initial stage in which a child mixes languages.

■ There can be a slow separation of the two languages.

■ One language system can influence the other.

■ One of the two languages usually becomes dominant.

■ There can be a rapid shift in use when the language in the environment changes. Even if the second language hasn't been spoken for some time, a bilingual speaker is able to just 'slot in' to the new environment.

Source: Arnberg (1987)

Another language will also open his mind to a wider variety of ideas, cultures and experiences. Imagine his delight at being able to read road signs in a foreign language, or his pleasure at being able to speak to Nonna (Grandma) in Italian, or read letters from her.

Language acquisition in young children may vary because either more than one language is being learnt or because of dialects in their parents' speech.

Sometimes a child learning two languages will mix them both within the same utterance before he is aware of having two languages in his environment. However, he gradually learns to separate them, and language mixing is unusual after four years of age.

Bilingual adults sometimes use 'code switching', a conscious or purposeful switching of the two languages within one sentence or between sentences. Code switching is skilful, showing that the speaker has a good grasp of both languages, but it can also be detrimental if used by parents in front of young children who are trying to learn the languages. Young children may become confused and be unsure which words belong to which language.

Because bilingual children may receive less exposure to each language, it may take them more time to achieve a similar language level to monolingual children. However, nearly all studies suggest that the bilingual child eventually 'catches up' after increased exposure.

HOW TO HELP YOUR BILINGUAL CHILD

The main processes involved in language learning are the same whether your child is learning one or more than one language. But do you teach both languages simultaneously or successively one after the other? Both methods can result in the child being successful with both languages. Parents might choose any of the strategies below to raise a child bilingually.

STRATEGIES FOR RAISING A CHILD BILINGUALLY

- An initial one-language strategy: your child learns one language first before another one is introduced.

- One person/one language method: Mum may decide to speak her native language while Dad uses English.

- A mixed language strategy: this is where any language may be used at any time.

- Speaking only the native minority language in your home while your child is exposed to the other language at preschool and other settings.

An initial one-language strategy, or sequential language development, will vary in its success according to when the second language is introduced in relation to the first language. Typically children have learnt much of their first language by about age three. It may be that they will learn the second language more easily because they already have a good grasp of not only the words of a language but also the way in which we use these words to communicate. It is your choice as to whether the second language is taught indirectly through exposure with peers at a preschool or more formally by attending special classes. In either case, it is important that your child is motivated to learn (especially if attending formal instruction) and also that your first language is not devalued in relation to the new language being learned.

When children are learning two languages simultaneously, research has shown they will quickly learn to attach each language to a particular person or purpose. So a young child might say 'drink' to his mother in her native Vietnamese language but use the word 'drink' when asking his English-speaking father.

You can also make a choice about the degree of bilingualism exposure and use. As with all language learning, it should be fun! Use singing books and role-playing activities to teach the minority language in your home. Other ideas include borrowing library books and subscribing to children's magazines in the minority language. Many storybook cassettes are available and video and television programs are also a great source of information and stimulation for learning.

Encourage your child's playgroup or kindergarten staff to become more interested in multiculturalism and the fostering of bilingualism. At the kindergarten you can display signs and labelled posters in various languages. You and other bilingual parents could go to the kindergarten and have fun teaching-sessions with all the children. The children will love learning to count in four different languages or to sing a nursery rhyme in German.

A child's English language development may also be affected by variations in the dialects to which he is exposed. A dialect is a pattern of speaking associated with a specific group or place and is distinguished by its vocabulary, grammar and pronunciation. A common misconception with certain dialects is that they do not represent 'proper' English and therefore prejudices or biases may develop. In our very mobile and cosmopolitan world it is naive to label someone who speaks differently from you as being 'wrong'.

Dialect variations occur in all countries of the world. In Australia, for example, we have differences between the way people from the east coast states and South Australia speak. There are variations in vowel-sound pronunciations as well as in the vocabulary used. 'Bathers' will be used in Adelaide but 'togs' are used in Brisbane and 'cossies' are used in Sydney. All three words refer to the clothes we wear when we go swimming and none of them is incorrect, yet one of us is often laughed at and frowned upon when she says 'I'll put my togs on'.

Having our children exposed to different dialects will not impede their language development or their learning ability later at school. They will soon learn there is a standard version of English used in the classroom which is different from their non-standard dialect used at home. They will also learn that there is only one version of English in print so speaking a non-standard dialect at home will not stop them from learning standard English. If you think about it, our children are being exposed to different dialects every time they watch a movie on television or at the cinema.

Bilingual children with speech and language problems

What happens if you are a bilingual family and your child has a speech or language problem? Every situation is different and it really depends on the nature and severity of the problem. If a problem arises, we would encourage you to discuss it with a speech pathologist.

In cases where the child may just have some immaturity in sound development, there is no need to stop using either language. In some cases it may be advisable to encourage only the use of the majority language for a period of time until the child catches up.

There have been situations when a child has severe language problems and therefore needs to concentrate on just one language until his skills improve. This might mean discontinuing attendance at a non-English language school, for example, until English skills improve. If the problem is severe, chances are it is obvious in both languages.

Grandparents and other extended family members often become concerned when the child has to concentrate on one language. They feel the child will never learn enough of their native language to talk effectively with them. They need to be reassured that the child will learn the native language but maybe just not as early as they had hoped. Once the problem is sorted out in English, the child can then learn the other language. Often, all that is required is for the parents (who spend so much one-to-one time with the young child) to use English, ensuring he will be exposed to the other language at family gatherings.

If the child with a problem is in the care of a non-English speaker or a very poor English speaker a large part of the time, this needs to be discussed with your child's speech pathologist. If you, as a bilingual family, are at any time concerned about your child's speech and language we recommend you seek advice.

Extended family members often comfort the parents by telling them that it is 'just the two languages that are making the child slower to talk'. Sometimes this may be the case but usually a speech problem has nothing to do with the bilingual background. It is more beneficial to seek help rather than let the child's problem become worse so that you have regrets later on.

In spite of the risk of delay in development a very large percentage of young children learn more than one language without any problems and as a result reap the social and cultural gains that bilingualism has to offer.

Children need a model to copy when learning a new skill.

Each infant needs regular one-to-one time with the parent if language skills are to develop adequately.

TWINS — THE MORE THE MERRIER

If you have twins, you will already be aware of the day-to-day joys and hassles. You might have two for the price of one, but you also have twice the work and twice the exhaustion — hopefully it leads to twice the fun!

One in 60 births is twins and one in 200 is triplets (Australian Bureau of Statistics, 2000). These odds are increased with a strong family history or participation in artificial fertility programs. In this section we have used the term 'twins' as these are the most common multiple births, but of course the same advice applies to larger multiples!

Risks of delayed language development

There is a general belief multiple-birth children are more likely to have delayed speech and language than single-birth children. Some do but many do not. Discussions about language development in multiple-birth children may be likened to discussions about language development in children from bilingual backgrounds. Children from both groups are at risk of language delay but if they receive adequate and correct input from birth, the risk of a delay is minimised.

The risks of problems are evident from the beginning. The babies have to share a womb and possibly even a placenta. Pregnancies of multiple births are usually shorter and the babies are born with a lower weight than would be expected from a single baby. Being born prematurely and having a lower birth-weight is known to increase the chances of further medical complications. The second-born or additional babies born are also at greater risk of injury at birth.

Once born, twins continue to share parents' time and resources, which reduces the amount of interaction and opportunities for each child. While we could argue that the children spend more time socialising together, the evidence indicates that twin-to-twin interaction on it's own may not be enough to develop the child's language system. Parents of twins sometimes say 'They sit and chatter and amuse each other all day.' This may mean they are less demanding but it may also mean their language development is suffering as a result. Children need a model to copy when learning a new skill. If young twins spend much of their time alone together, they have only each other to copy. They are less exposed to the adult model, and, critically, they each have less exposure to the adult model *alone*. Each infant needs regular one-to-one time with a parent if language skills are to develop adequately. Easier said than done when there are two or more toddlers the same age running around!

Treating twins individually

It is not unusual for a twin who is more noisy, outgoing and demanding to get more attention than the quieter one. However, we must be wary of classifying them as 'the dominant one' and 'the quiet one'. This creates stereotypes and leads us to have different expectations for each child. We will, in time, always expect the more dominant child to say more and the quieter child to say less.

Furthermore, because twins usually relate to each other so well, they may not be expected to be as good as a single child in relating to others. The pressure is therefore not as great to make themselves understood and express their thoughts clearly. For this reason too, parents should try to have one-to-one time with each child. If this is not possible to organise, try to address each child individually by always directing questions and comments to each one rather than to both at once.

Try not to anticipate their needs, either jointly or individually, but always give them the chance to express their own needs. Remember that you are doing this not only for the sake of their language development but also for the sake of their social development. Sending one twin to a friend's place to play gives each the opportunity to interact alone and not rely on the other. It also gives the parent more one-to-one time with the child who stays home.

Often, if twins have been delayed in their language development this has been accepted as a 'normal part of being a twin'. This need not be the case. It is important to remember that twins and other multiple-birth children have the same potential for good speech and language as other children and we must not expect otherwise just because there is more than one.

Research has shown that, on average, twins are six to eight months later in saying their first words, and when they start school, twins (especially boys) are six to nine months behind single-born children in their overall language skills. Tests have shown their vocabulary to be more limited, hence the risk of reading problems is increased. A delay in language development can result in a delay in imaginative play and also in social behaviour towards peers and teachers.

Twins are the same as single children, in that early speech and language problems can lead to later problems with reading, writing and spelling. Therefore early and appropriate language input is important. If you are concerned at any time, contact a speech pathologist.

9 Using speech to encourage positive behaviour

We don't wish to become bogged down with the subject of discipline. Discipline is an issue for all parents at some stage and there are many books which already cover this topic thoroughly.

However, your child's behaviours, both positive and negative, are forms of communication. Hence you can use your own communication skills and your knowledge of your child's language ability to encourage positive behaviour, to avoid potentially difficult situations and to manage your child when he is misbehaving.

As with other aspects of development, the teaching and learning of appropriate behaviour begins at birth. At first, babies need to feel secure and require lots of reassurance. But you need to find a healthy balance: you don't want to control your child so much that he becomes too frightened to try new activities and experiment with new ideas.

No! No! No!
How many different ways can you ask your child
to stop an activity without using 'no'?

When one of our children was just beginning to enjoy splashing in the water he had grommets (tubes) inserted in his ears. To prevent him getting an infection others would panic, shout or grab him (sometimes all three at once!) every time water crept up near his ears. This was so successful at encouraging fear of water that it took six years and a lot of hard work for him to overcome this fear.

It is very important that you give your child as much (or more) attention when he is happy and playing well as when he is crying or naughty. Your child needs to know which behaviour is the appropriate one — how is he supposed to know unless you tell him?

Try to find something to praise about your child's behaviours every hour of the day. Some days you might feel you have to look hard to find it, but you will. Try:

'Good boy, did you do that all by yourself? Clever boy!'

or

'That's nice playing, you two. You are sharing nicely together.'

Remember it takes them time to learn, and children need reminders given in a positive way over and over again.

Toddlers are inquisitive and often not in control of their behaviour. They have to learn to take turns and share, or to wait. Toddlers love to copy you, so watch your own behaviour. It's not fair to have one rule for the children and another for the grown-ups.

This is also the time when your child greatly increases his use of the word 'no'. After all, he has heard it so many times! It might be possible to prevent such a negative response by limiting your own use of the word. How many different ways can you ask your child to stop an activity without using 'no'?

When your child becomes mobile and starts talking, you may find your expectations increase enormously. If we demand too much of our children we may find an increase in temper tantrums is the result. We all get frustrated if we find a task too hard or are expected to 'perform' in a different situation. These feelings are increased when a well-meaning friend lets us know we are failing.

Yes! Yes! Yes! Good Girl ... Good Boy ...
Try to find something to praise about your child's behaviours every hour of the day.

Your toddler will only grasp the basics of an activity. He may in fact be trying to be helpful when he throws his china plate onto the floor — didn't he see you throw his plastic cup into the kitchen sink only this morning? Someone needs to explain the difference between china and plastic and between the sink and the floor!

Your child eventually has to learn that there are different ways of doing something. You may turn a blind eye to him drinking his soup straight from the bowl at home, but it is not acceptable when you are out in company.

If we use our language wisely we can try to phrase our requests positively rather than concentrate on the negative behaviour. We want to teach our children the appropriate behaviour, so just

INSTEAD OF	HOW ABOUT TRYING
Oh, do stop whining.	I'll listen when you use a normal voice.
Don't slam the door when you go out!	Can you shut the door gently, please? Thank you.
Stop shouting!	Use a quiet voice, please.

INSTEAD OF	HOW ABOUT TRYING
Isn't there something you're supposed to do?	Please turn off the TV. Thank you.
Why is the Lego all over the floor?	Put your Lego back in the box, please.
Stop interrupting. It's very irritating.	Please wait until I've finished.
Stop doing that, you dirty boy.	Stop spitting right now.
Stop! That's not where the cornflakes go.	Put the cornflakes in the bowl.

complaining about his irritating behaviour doesn't tell him what he should be doing.

If you want to try to change your child's behaviour make sure you give a clear message. Let him know what you want him to do and possibly why. A calm, firm voice is more effective with a young child than shouting. A screaming voice conveys the message that you are angry. You may find that your child is so upset by the atmosphere shouting creates that he doesn't even listen to the message.

Try avoiding commands or questions that can be answered with 'no'.

Most parents eventually want their children to become independent: to make choices for themselves and to reason why they make a certain choice. Being able to choose helps your child realise that what he thinks *is* important and that he *can* influence an event or activity. Children need practice at this. Wherever possible give simple choices:

'*Let's go to the shop. Shall we walk or go by car?*'

If you do give a choice, you need to respect the response. If he chooses to go by car only to have you overriding his decision by saying:

'No, it's such a nice day I think we will walk',

where was the choice for your child?

Following on from this, make sure you're not giving a choice when in fact there isn't one. It's inviting a tantrum to ask your child what he would like for lunch when you only have peanut butter. Similarly, a question such as:

'Are you going to come and have your bath now?'

is unnecessary if in fact there is no choice. A positively phrased statement is more appropriate:

'It's bath time now.'

Treat your child with the respect you give to any adult. If you can tell your child what to do and expect an immediate response, then perhaps it should work both ways. If you can demand:

'Come on! We're late. Get into the car now!'

then perhaps your child has the right to demand:

'Get me a drink now!'

Using 'please' and 'thank you' will teach him a polite approach.

Giving advance warning of a change of activity can prevent tantrums as well as communicate your intentions to your child. Imagine watching your favourite TV program and your partner walks in and demands:

'Turn the TV off. I want to go out for a drink!'

Impressed? Your child is a person with feelings too, not an object to be ordered about.

A warning will also prepare your child to adjust to a change in circumstances:

'Three more throws and I have to get dinner ready.'
'When the advertisements come on, we have to go to the shops.
We need some food to eat.'

Try to help your child to understand and take the consequences of his actions. If your child makes such a fuss that you decide to let him wear his socks and sandals on a rainy day, then he has to put up with wet feet and not expect a change of footwear to magically appear when he feels uncomfortable.

Constant threats are not helpful. Constant warnings might scare your child: 'Be careful, you'll fall', and 'I told you so' when he does fall contributes nothing but bad feeling to the situation.

Consistent handling is extremely important. Not only should one person be consistent but parents need to agree on management or the child will learn how to manipulate the situation and play one partner off against the other.

Be sure of your facts before making a stand — the offence may not be as serious as it first seems and once you have made a decision on how to handle the situation, you will have to stick with it. If you keep changing your mind or 'giving in', your child will learn that it's well worth his nagging and keeping up the pressure. By doing it, he usually gets what he wants.

Consistency will help your child learn the rules and know where his boundaries are. When you say 'no' make sure you mean 'no' and not 'maybe' or 'I'm open to persuasion'.

Feelings and self-esteem

Young children need help to recognise and understand their feelings, as well as the feelings of others.

INSTEAD OF	HOW ABOUT TRYING
You are naughty to throw toys about the room.	Toys are for playing, not for throwing. Don't throw the toys. Something might get broken.
You are so naughty. Why do you kick other children?	Kicking hurts. You are not to do it.

Even when your child is very young, give a name to his mood. If someone takes his toy, acknowledge that he is angry. Let him know that you understand:

'You are angry because that boy took your ball away.'

If there is a dispute with another child, encourage him to express his feelings and explain what has upset him:

'That hurt when you pinched me.'

Make sure your own feelings are clarified. If you are upset, let your child know it is not his fault:

'Sorry I shouted, Mummy is so tired today.'

Your child needs to know that whatever your mood or whatever the behaviour, you still love him. He will be secure knowing this. Never threaten to withdraw affection. This is both cruel and dangerous. When your child has behaved badly, make it very clear it is the behaviour which is the problem not the child. The slight shift of emphasis is important for your child's self-esteem.

Encourage your child to feel pleased with his *own* behaviour and successes. He doesn't need to be completely dependent on other people for praise:

'You read that all by yourself. You must be so proud of yourself.'

Your message can help develop your child's positive self-esteem.

Handling difficult behaviours

When our children are misbehaving, most of us do not stop to think — we just react. It might be easier said than done, but try to stop and think before you respond. What is your child trying to communicate to you? Why is he doing it?

Ask yourself some of the following questions, and remember that a child's age and developmental level may make your responses different for different children.

Stop and Think
Why am I unhappy with this behaviour?
Am I overreacting?
Why is my child doing this?
What will help my child learn not to do it again?

WHY AM I UNHAPPY WITH THIS BEHAVIOUR?

How serious is the situation? Is it physically dangerous? Did it hurt someone?

Do you think your child understands you do not approve of the behaviour? Or is it time to start teaching some simple rules like: 'No hitting, it hurts.'

Throughout this book we have referred to expectations. Consider whether you have appropriate expectations for your child. Is it possible they are too high? Are you expecting your two-year-old to behave like your neighbour's four-year-old?

Before you respond to your child's behaviour, remember you want to communicate a message to your child. Your response needs to be appropriate for the behaviour. If you are shouting and screaming all the time, then your child may find it so predictable he starts to ignore your voice — your shouting may become yet another background noise and lose its effect. In a dangerous situation, your child's immediate response may save a life. Say, for instance, his ball runs onto the road and he tries to run after it. You will shout at him to stop. Hopefully your child will realise from your voice that this is important and stop.

Perhaps for a more routine situation like books all over the floor, a positive comment along the lines already discussed would be more appropriate:

'Can you help me put all these books back on the shelf?'

The best strategy for dealing with poor behaviour is to encourage and teach positive alternative behaviour.

AM I OVERREACTING?

If you are, then why? Are you tired or unwell? If you are, don't set yourself and your family numerous or unrealistic goals for the day. Take it easy — go to the park, get a takeaway dinner.

WHY IS MY CHILD DOING THIS?

Is he bored and seeking attention? Have you had a busy day? Is your child letting you know he would like some of your time?

Is he frustrated? Is the activity too difficult or does he need some help? You may be able to ease the frustration by breaking down the activity into smaller steps. Sometimes frustration may arise because in fact the task is too easy. Just because he enjoyed doing the activity once, doesn't mean he wants to keep doing it.

WHAT WILL HELP MY CHILD LEARN NOT TO DO IT AGAIN?

When you do discipline your child, you want him to learn how to manage himself more effectively and cope with the world. Listed below are some general tactics. If you would like to investigate this further, there is some suggested reading at the end of this book.

Ignoring the incident This can be easier said than done. Any parent who has a whining child around will know how difficult this is, but it can be effective. Ignoring only works if your child is seeking your attention and the behaviour, such as using 'bad words' or 'words to shock', can be ignored. Not commenting can often defuse the situation. Toddler tantrums may occur less frequently if they are ignored.

Distracting him The success of this method depends on your child's age. Older children are more difficult to distract, but it's relatively easy in the baby/toddler group. Try to be realistic. Expecting your toddler to share can be unrealistic, but finding another toy of interest — especially if it's similar — can be helpful. Sometimes you may be able to distract both children from the offending object. Perhaps you could suddenly see a cat in the garden!

Prevention When your child becomes mobile you'll find that he gets into everything. You can remove your child from the cause of trouble, but it's often more appropriate to rearrange the environment to avoid trouble occurring in the first place. It may be impossible for your newly standing child to ignore the temptation of a dangling tablecloth!

Giving simple reasons Offering a simple reason or setting the rules ('Hitting hurts, no hitting.') may be far more effective than shouting. For very young children, using an exaggerated expression in your voice will help:

'Oh! Hot! Hurts!'

Time out Your child can be put into 'time out' by removing him and placing him in a situation (such as his bedroom or a corner of the room) where he is given no attention at all. Or you might leave the room yourself.

Time out gives you and your child a chance to calm down and save face. You'll need to explain it in advance — don't just spring it on him. And make sure he knows when time out finishes — when a clock rings, for example.

For a small child, it's best to keep it very brief. It is best to use time out only for behaviours that you just cannot ignore.

Punishment Punishment in the form of hitting is not recommended at all. It communicates the message that it's all right to be aggressive and hit someone if you don't like what he is doing. Remember that punishment is not discipline but a sign that discipline has been unsuccessful. When it is really necessary, punishment should never be humiliating and once administered, the incident should be forgotten.

The best strategy for dealing with poor behaviour is to encourage and teach positive alternative behaviour.

10 What is a speech pathologist / speech therapist?

A speech pathologist, speech and language therapist or speech therapist are actually all the same profession but the name varies from country to country so it depends which term you are more familiar with. Just make sure that your therapist has a university degree in dealing with communication disorders and is not an elocution teacher working beyond their training. A qualified therapist has had extensive training in normal child language and general development as well as psychology, biology, audiology and communication disorders to name but a few areas. It is not unheard of for very young children to be receiving 'therapy' for so-called problems, many of which are part of normal development and would have disappeared with maturity. At the same time, children with serious problems may not be receiving experienced expert attention.

A speech pathologist works with anyone, children or adults, who has some sort of problem communicating. They also work on any problem that will ultimately affect communication. For example, speech pathologists work with children with feeding difficulties, even newborn babies, because it is this early use of the oral muscles that strengthens and tones them for later use in speech.

Q WHAT WILL THE SPEECH PATHOLOGIST BE ABLE TO DO?

The speech pathologist will be able to look in detail at your child's communication skills. They need to work out if indeed there is a problem and if so what is its cause. They also need to decide if your child would benefit from seeing any other professional to help complete the picture of your child's strengths and weaknesses. There are four main areas they will work through:

1 Assessment Initially the speech pathologist will need to get some idea of your child's current level of development. They will carry out a range of formal and informal tests to gain some idea as to his speech, language and general skills. (These tests are explained in detail in the response to 'What skills will be evaluated?' on page 159.)

2 Diagnosis The more information the speech pathologist has, the easier it is for them to formulate an opinion as to the diagnosis. Once a diagnosis has been made then the steps on how to tackle the problem can be decided. A report is usually written so that you can absorb the information and follow up any further queries you may have.

3 Treatment With the parents, the speech pathologist will formulate a treatment plan. This may vary from a home/school program, weekly input or intensive therapy. There is no set formula, every child is different and the program will be geared to your child's specific needs. Do be honest about your family's set-up and routines. It will not benefit anyone if the program can't be carried out. One of our husbands travels a great deal and we know first-hand how as a single parent it is hard to find the extra time required to practise at home.

4 Counselling The speech pathologist will have experience with a whole range of problems and concerns and will be able to direct and guide you to any other professionals, resources or support that may be beneficial.

Q MY CHILD HAS QUITE CLEAR SPEECH SO WHY HAS HE BEEN REFERRED TO A SPEECH PATHOLOGIST?

Children with problems with poor clarity of speech actually form a very small percentage of a speech pathologist's caseload.

The speech pathologist's training encompasses all aspects of communication and all the associated skills required for communication, including:

- speech;
- oral skills, including muscles for eating;
- writing;
- symbol;
- gestures.

Q WHAT SKILLS WILL BE EVALUATED?

An assessment by a speech pathologist will vary depending on the nature of your child's problem. If the problem is a lisp the speech pathologist will not spend hours evaluating skills irrelevant to the problem. On the other hand, some problems may put your child at risk in other areas of development and screening may be appropriate as a preventative measure. Here is a list of the areas that the speech pathologist may need to cover. It is quite long, but the combination will vary depending on the reason for referral and the results of the initial assessment.

Developmental history This gives the speech pathologist an idea as to how your child's speech and language skills are developing in relation to other aspects of their development.

Family history Many speech and language problems are inherited although not necessarily with an identical pattern. Knowing the family history gives the speech pathologist some idea of any risk factors. In this way a child whose skills are just within the normal range but has a family history of language/literacy problems may be monitored more closely. Sometimes parents don't know there is a family history until they speak to Grandma about the visit. Many times parents come back to us and say they have just discovered a family member had learning and literacy problems.

Medical history A range of health conditions or illnesses can influence speech and language development. This may vary from frequent upper respiratory infections to inpatient-stays in hospital.

Informal assessment of general behaviour and parent–child relationship This is nothing for the parents to worry about. Don't feel your parenting skills are being evaluated and judged. Some children work better than others with their parents. At times, parents of children with significant language problems may have to modify their approach to help their child. This does not imply that their approach is incorrect but rather is a suggestion as to how to help the child with problems and to aid communication between them.

Imitation Your child's ability to copy what he has seen or heard will influence his development and will certainly influence the approach to treatment.

Hearing This is perhaps an obvious area to assess, and is often done informally. However, if there are language difficulties or an unusual speech pattern, there should always be a formal evaluation. One four-year-old client was extremely bright and articulate but had slushy speech. She seemed so sharp that her hearing was not questioned too seriously until she insisted that her speech sounded exactly like the speech pathologist. It turned out that this delightful little girl had quite a significant hearing loss but was so bright she had managed to compensate by lip reading and picking up other clues. An audiologist should evaluate hearing.

Comprehension The understanding of speech and language can be further broken down into the separate skills required.

Attention and listening. Your child may have excellent hearing but is not able to put to good use what he has heard.

Auditory memory and discrimination. Can your child remember what they have seen or heard or discriminate between small differences?

Understanding of spoken language. This sounds obvious but some parents are surprised when their child presents with problems in this area. They felt that their child understood everything. However, bright children are very capable of picking up clues from their environment. Of course you are going out when you have your coat on! Try and sit in on the formal testing if you can. This will make it much easier when you are discussing the results later.

Understanding of gesture, intonation and tone. We actually place a lot of importance on the way people speak. If you were told 'You've done a great job' by someone using an angry voice, would you trust the words or the tone? Which does your child respond to, the word or tone?

Understanding of written language. This would be evaluated in the older child with literacy problems.

Language production (expressive language)

Mode used. By what means does your child communicate? Some children are so very good at gesturing that they can get away with limited spoken communication, others may point and grunt.

Syntactic complexity. What level of grammatical structures is your child using and is it at an appropriate level for his age? Is the development following a normal pattern but at a slower rate or is the pattern unusual?

Semantic complexity. This area looks at vocabulary and how the child can use words to convey meaning.

Abnormal qualities to spoken language. Is the language stereotyped? Does it sound strange in any way?

Social situation. Can your child use the right type of communication for the situation he is in?

Amount of communication. Is the quantity of speech used appropriate for his age?

Narrative. How adept is your child at conveying information and using his communication to solve problems and formulate solutions.

Pragmatic skills. This area investigates the overall ability to communicate appropriately. Does he pick up cues from his peers?

Sound production and use of rules How clear is your child's speech for his chronological age? Sometimes children's speech is clear in some situations but not in others. Perhaps he can imitate your production of the word but is unable to produce it spontaneously in his own conversation.

Rhythm and rate of speech How fluent is your child's speech? Is the way he is speaking so disruptive that the listener is concentrating on *how* he is speaking rather than *what* he is saying. This is of course typical of the stutterer or clutterer.

Phonation Some children develop croaky voices as they get older; this may be due to constant shouting and what is called an 'abuse' of the vocal cords. In consultation with a speech pathologist the child may have to learn how to use his voice without causing this damage.

Q MY CHILD HAS BEEN ASSESSED BY A SPEECH PATHOLOGIST
BUT WHAT DO ALL THE NUMBERS ON THE TEST RESULTS REFER TO?

Once a speech pathologist has assessed your child you should receive a written report. Hopefully you will have the opportunity to discuss the results. If you haven't received a report but would like one, contact the speech pathologist and request one.

If your child has been observed there will be a description of the observations. But it is likely that some form of standardised test has been carried out. Possibly different tests have been used to evaluate different aspects of communication skills. These tests provide information as to how your child has performed in relation to other children of the same age. Before they are put into general use, tests are carried out on many, many children to find out what is typical at various ages. This information is collated and enables a comparison to be made. Some parents worry because their child doesn't know the examiner very well or the testing situation is strange. However, these tests have been standardised on children in similar circumstances. The speech pathologist should also be familiar with working with children with problems and putting them at ease. The most common terms you will come across are 'age equivalent', 'percentile' and 'standard score'.

Age equivalent This compares your child's development with his chronological age (CA). If your child is five years and two months old but his language skills are one year behind, then his CA is five years and two months and his age equivalent (AE) is four years and two months. His language is comparable to a child of four years and two months old.

Percentile This enables a comparison in terms of percentages. Most children score between the 25th and 75th percentile, that is between 25 and 75 per cent of children score at this level. If your child scores in the 91st percentile it means that he is better in this area than 91 per cent of his age group. Similarly if your child scores in the 9th percentile it means that he is stronger in this area than 9 per cent of his peers but 91 per cent are stronger than he is.

Standard score This varies from test to test, but is based on a system whereby 100 or sometimes 10 is average. The average range also varies from test to test. Usually between 80 and 120 (or 8 and 12) is considered an average range. Scores below 80 or 8 might be investigated further.

The test should describe the area of communication that was assessed. However, if you have any queries or concerns regarding the results or you are not sure about the vocabulary used you should not hesitate to contact the professional concerned to clarify the situation.

Q I UNDERSTAND MY CHILD HAS A PROBLEM.
WHAT KIND OF TREATMENT WILL BE OFFERED?

Many parents telephone us giving details of their child's problem and requesting information about how much therapy will be required. Unfortunately, it is not possible to answer that question without seeing the child. There is no set therapy; children are unique and likewise their family circumstances are unique. However, the speech pathologist will take into account:

- the severity of the problem;
- the nature of the problem;

- who will be working with the child at home and/or at school;
- practical issues, such as how easy is it to get to the speech pathologist;
- the value of withdrawing a child from class as opposed to staying within the class;
- the time they have available to treat the problem;
- sometimes, unfortunately, even the cost.

Children can be seen individually or in a group. If your child is being seen within a group, the other members of the group should be chosen with care to make sure that the problem is being tackled and that the children are compatible.

Individual sessions may be anywhere from 30 minutes to one hour long depending on your child's concentration span and the aim of the session. This may be once or twice a week or once a month or term. If your child is being seen less frequently, sessions may need to be longer to enable the speech pathologist to catch up on any changes or progress since the last visit, carry out any therapy and discuss with you any program which needs to be carried out prior to the next consultation.

Once therapy is completed it is worthwhile following up with a review appointment a few months later to make sure that the skills have been maintained without the ongoing support.

Q MY CHILD NEEDS TO SEE A SPEECH PATHOLOGIST. HOW DO I GO ABOUT FINDING ONE?

Parents who are concerned about their child's progress are usually encouraged to speak to their GP or the child's teacher first. While this may be a valuable beginning, a referral from a medical practitioner is not required for parents to take their child to see a speech pathologist either in the public or private sectors.

Usually you can just telephone and give your child's details over the phone. Many speech pathologists, especially in hospitals and community centres, have waiting lists, so put your child's name down as soon as possible. An appointment can always be cancelled if it is not needed when the time comes.

Speech pathologists in private practice may be listed in the Yellow Pages, or your family doctor or child health worker may be able to recommend one. Private practitioners may offer convenient hours and personalised care along with special expertise. There is a cost involved, however some rebate may be possible through your private health fund.

Speech pathologists also work in community health centres, education departments, children's services offices and kindergartens. These are free services but many have long waiting lists or limited services available.

Wherever you take your child, do find out about the speech pathologist's experience and whether or not she provides the kinds of services you are looking for. You may think twice about taking your child to see someone who has only ever worked with adult stroke patients! Not all speech pathologists work the same way so check out what services are available and how easy or not it is to access them.

If a parent is concerned, they really should not feel they are wasting anyone's time. They should go to the professional who specialises in that area. If a doctor or other professional has advised you to wait and see but you are still concerned do go ahead and contact a speech pathologist directly. As speech pathologists, we can assure you that we would much rather tell a parent not to worry and give some suggestions than be concerned that the child has sought help much too late for therapy to be truly effective. Unfortunately most of us have seen school-aged children for the first time who could have benefited from preschool input, but the parents were advised, by another professional, that their child would probably grow out of the problem. Equally, many people feel that once a child is speaking relatively competently there is no further need for a speech pathologist. However, the way the child uses these communication skills to survive and thrive both academically and socially is just as important. One of our children has a kidney disorder and we would not be comfortable with anyone but a specialist dealing with his disorder, so if you are concerned about any learning difficulties seek advice from the appropriate specialist. In our experience a parent's gut feelings are usually correct and should not be readily dismissed.

11 Common questions about talking

Q HOW WILL I RECOGNISE IF MY CHILD
HAS A SPEECH OR LANGUAGE PROBLEM?

As parents we often learn what is normal or appropriate development from past experience and our observations of other children. In the case of the first-born child this is more difficult. Below is a very basic guide as to when it would be best for you to seek advice from a speech pathologist. Do refer also to the relevant sections within this book, especially Chapters 2, 3 and 10.

Seek advice if your child:

- is not using some single words by 18 months;
- is not putting words together by age two;
- is not using three- to four-word sentences by age three to three-and-a-half;

- is using immature sentences;
- is hard to understand by age three;
- is making sound errors well beyond the appropriate age;
- is not responding to sounds;
- does not seem to listen to and understand instructions;
- is using many non-specific words as if he can't remember the names;
- has a poor memory for names and information;
- has poor understanding of a range of concepts including colour, size, number and time;
- gets confused when telling a story or giving information; information may be confused or hard to work out;
- has poor development of problem-solving skills;
- is slow to take off with reading and has very weak phonological awareness skills;
- is using a nasal, loud, jerky or hoarse voice;
- is so hesitant or repetitive when talking that it makes the listener anxious.

Q WHAT POSSIBLE REASON COULD THERE BE FOR MY CHILD'S SPEECH PROBLEM?

Finding the exact cause of a problem may be difficult. Some speech problems and learning difficulties can be inherited, like many other developmental disorders, however, the following are the most common causes:

- Hearing loss — even a temporary loss may create a delay in speech development.
- Language and/or speech delay — perhaps the child is just immature in the area of language but is progressing through the appropriate stages.
- Language disorder — sometimes a child with normal intellectual ability can have difficulty understanding what is said to him or expressing himself.
- Oral deformity — such as a cleft palate.
- Poor oral coordination — some children have difficulty

learning how to coordinate their mouth movements to produce speech.

- Intellectual disability.

Unfortunately we often don't know why some children have difficulties and others don't. Some children will make rapid progress on a home-based program while others require intensive professional input over many months. The earlier they start, the better the outcome.

Q DOES MY CHILD HAVE HEARING PROBLEMS?

Normal hearing is a prerequisite for speech development. Early childhood check-ups will screen your child's hearing and we recommend that you attend these annually until he starts school. While hearing problems are not the cause of most of the speech difficulties we see, early detection means early prevention and treatment.

Signs of hearing problems include:

- not paying attention when being spoken to;
- constantly asking for what is said to be repeated;
- mispronouncing words slightly by confusing sounds;
- behavioural problems;
- frequent upper-respiratory infections;
- little use of speech;
- staring at people's mouths when they talk.

If you are at any time concerned about your child's hearing, have an audiologist assess him. This is a more detailed evaluation than the quick screening test given at the annual childhood check-ups. Audiologists work at children's hospitals, government-operated hearing assessment clinics and in private-practice clinics. This evaluation is carried out in a specially designed soundproof booth and a skilled audiologist will adjust the presentation of the test to suit the age and language level of your child.

Q CAN EAR, NOSE AND THROAT PROBLEMS AFFECT SPEECH AND LANGUAGE DEVELOPMENT?

Ear, nose and throat (ENT) problems are very common in childhood and may account for repeated minor illnesses as well as frequent visits to doctors and even admissions to hospital.

Repeated attacks of hay fever, obstructed breathing, sinusitis, tonsillitis and middle-ear infections can contribute to poor general development and reduced mental alertness. Children with recurrent episodes of tonsillitis, ear infections or sinusitis often show a lack of appetite and therefore sometimes have a slower rate of physical growth. They may seem to be always tired and listless and this will affect their rate of learning.

A child who is ill may not feel well enough to do much talking, or well-meaning adults may encourage a more passive behaviour which allows the child's needs to be met without having to talk. For instance, every time the child cries he may be given a drink immediately without having to ask for it.

Many children suffer from upper-respiratory and middle-ear infections and do not complain about the pain. This may go unnoticed during the early preschool years and during that time the child's hearing may have been fluctuating. If this happened often enough at a critical time in his development, speech and language can be delayed. Therefore, the importance of attending the health clinic for regular checks — which include hearing tests — cannot be stressed enough.

Babies start to hear during the last months of pregnancy and are born with full hearing. A baby of six months will turn its head to locate a sound. The onset of the first words at around 12 months may indicate to the parents that hearing is adequate for speech and language development. However, this situation may change as a result of middle-ear infections or other illnesses. Given the critical time for speech and language development is the first three to five years, it is essential to monitor your child's health. It is not only how often your child has a middle-ear infection that can affect his development, but also the duration and severity of each infection and how quickly medical treatment is sought. Speech production is affected because the child reproduces speech in the muffled and distorted way it is heard. Language skills can be delayed in several ways: the child might be late saying their first words and putting words together; they might have a smaller vocabulary; and their grammar skills may be slower to develop. Therefore, if at any time you have doubts about your infant's hearing, take him to your health clinic or to your doctor. A screening test will show whether further testing is required.

It is important to be aware of the difference between hearing and listening. Some preschoolers are simply stubborn and may refuse to listen. If you examine a variety of situations you will notice that your child may not respond to you when you ask him to pick up his toys but he will respond if he hears you rattle the biscuit barrel. Such a child does not have a hearing problem — he is just being a 'selective listener'!

Q MY CHILD GETS LOTS OF MIDDLE-EAR INFECTIONS. IS THIS A PROBLEM? WHAT CAN THE DOCTOR DO ABOUT IT?

Middle-ear infection (*otitis media*) is one of the most common childhood illnesses and develops when bacteria or a virus infects the middle part of the ear just behind the eardrum. It is sometimes referred to as 'glue ear'. This affects the normal function of the eustachian tube, preventing air from reaching the middle ear and excess fluid from draining away.

Frequent middle-ear infections, especially between the critical period from birth to four years of age, may disrupt the development of speech and language.

These infections are usually treated with antibiotics, but your child may be referred to an ear, nose and throat specialist if the problem keeps occurring and/or is very severe. It may be necessary for grommets (small tubes) to be inserted into the eardrum to enable fluid to drain away and to reduce pressure.

Your child may well 'grow out' of middle-ear infections but due to their effect on speech and language development they should be monitored carefully.

Q WHAT IS THE EFFECT OF SUCKING DUMMIES, THUMBS AND BOTTLES?

Sucking is a basic physiological function which plays a role in developing breathing coordination and speech. It helps develop a sense of touch and sight and helps in the development of the teeth, jaw and facial muscles. Most babies are soothed by sucking whether it's on the breast, bottle, hand or dummy.

Sucking is fun and makes a baby feel good. Although there is an anti-dummy movement, if presented with the choice of an irritable baby or using a dummy, perhaps like us you'll choose the latter!

However, be careful not to use a dummy as a plug to keep the baby's mouth closed and him quiet. Constant use can lead to passive children who are only happy when they have something in their mouths. It may also produce children who have no desire to talk. It's easier to say nothing and just point to a cup than to take the dummy out and say 'Drink please.'

If a child tries to talk with the dummy in his mouth, remind him that you would like to be able to understand him and that it's easier to talk without a dummy.

A dummy should not be used to distract a child who is seeking adult attention and involvement in an activity. It is not a substitute for parent–child interaction.

You might wonder if there is ever a 'right' time to take the dummy away from the child. It is a good idea to be guided by your child to some extent — when you sense he is only using it out of habit take it away and see what happens. If a baby starts to spit the dummy out or push the tongue forward when sucking on it, the use of it should be questioned.

If you are concerned and want your infant to stop using it, then try not replacing the dummy next time it is lost! However, we all know that is not as easy as it sounds. Rather than making it a battle ground, try explaining that you have lost the dummy and look everywhere for it with your child helping. Make sure they have all been thrown away so there is no chance of finding one! Use your child's language ability. 'Silly Mummy lost the dummies. What would you like to take to bed? Teddy?' At the outside, try to 'lose' the dummy by the time your child is two. You might then suggest, when the last one is 'lost', that shops don't sell dummies for big children of two or more!

Thumb-sucking is also worth mentioning at this point and much of what is said about the dummy can apply to thumb-sucking as well. Prolonged thumb-sucking can interfere with the development of your child's teeth. It may also cause the child's tongue to rest in a more forward position in the mouth which can lead to abnormal swallowing patterns, tongue-thrusting and poor production of some speech sounds, as in a lisp. We have seen some terrible situations where children of six years and older have very significant dental problems and are still sucking their thumb. Self-esteem is low because of teasing about their teeth and speech, and they will require a lot of orthodontic work for several years.

Like the dummy, reminding the child of his level of maturity can often stop thumb-sucking. This works particularly well if there is a younger baby in the household and the elder child can see that only babies and not 'big children' suck their thumbs or use a dummy.

Or try talking about a 'naughty thumb' (rather than a 'naughty child'). 'Can you be the boss and teach the thumb not to go in your mouth?' is an approach worth trying. The older child might like to bandage the 'naughty thumb', so that he is reminded by the feel of the bandages to take the thumb away. Praise him for being a good teacher when you see him without the thumb in his mouth.

There are many different techniques to try (such as nail paint), but working positively with your child should be much more successful than making him feel inferior.

Bottle-feeding is meant to be like breastfeeding in that the infant gets regular good sucking practice. The type of teat is therefore important and should not allow the infant to just gulp to get his milk. Hard teats tend to pull a baby's jaw in narrower and this forces him to open his lips and breathe through his mouth. This may result in the top teeth being pushed forward or the development of a tongue-thrusting pattern. As stated earlier, both of these can cause problems with speech development. Because of this, it is advisable to make the transition to cup drinking by the age of 12 months.

Recent research has shown a renewed increase of teeth cavities in toddlers as a result of them being given drinks containing sugar in their bottle. Many parents use the bottle as an easy way to calm their child, distract him, get him off to sleep or simply to keep the child busy. As with the dummy, the child just learns to have his needs satisfied by drinking. It is astounding to think some parents put their four-year-plus child to sleep with a bottle. Yes it does matter! We recently heard of a five-year-old who had all her upper teeth removed because of decay. Imagine the effect of this on eating and speaking, not to mention social interaction.

Q THE SPEECH PATHOLOGIST SAYS MY CHILD HAS A TONGUE-THRUST. WHAT DOES THIS MEAN? WHY IS THE DENTIST CONCERNED?

Tongue-thrusting is a way of swallowing. In normal swallowing, the back teeth are in alignment while the tongue pushes up and then pulls back. In tongue-thrusting, the tongue pushes forward against the upper front teeth or protrudes between the teeth.

All babies use a thrusting swallow at first, but should change to a normal swallow during the preschool years. Some, however, don't make the change, for a number of reasons including:

- prolonged thumb- or dummy-sucking;
- enlarged tonsils or adenoids;
- allergies and nasal congestion;
- very high, narrow palate;
- poor muscle coordination.

Tongue-thrusting is frequently associated with a lisp. The dentist will be concerned because the constant pressure of the tongue against the teeth can contribute to dental problems or malformation.

A speech pathologist can help your child to retrain his tongue posture.

Q WHEN IS DRIBBLING A PROBLEM?

Dribbling is a normal part of development, especially from four to six months. This is usually the time when baby is ready for eating solids. Copious dribbling can also be a sign of teething, thrush or a mouth infection.

Dribbling can occur as a child is learning a new motor skill and later, in the 15-month to 24-month period, they may dribble when concentrating in play or when drawing.

Some children do continue to have problems with dribbling in association with other oral problems. Obviously good control of the tongue, lips and jaw is necessary for speech development. Some children present as being sensitive around the mouth area and lack awareness of their oral muscles. They may dribble, mouth breathe, dislike being touched around the mouth, not eat solid foods and be generally fussy eaters.

To help infants gain greater control of their tongue and lips, you can play games involving the mouth from a young age. Blow raspberries, blow bubbles, blow out candles and blow and drink through straws. All of these activities will make the child more aware of his mouth and strengthen the muscles. If you are concerned, consult a speech pathologist for advice.

Q COULD MY CHILD BE TONGUE-TIED?

A tongue-tie (or anklyoglossia) is where the skin connecting the tongue tip to the bottom of the mouth is very short. In other words, the skin under the tongue is too close to the tongue tip. A tongue-tie limits tongue movements during speaking and swallowing, and this can affect the production of some speech sounds and the development of teeth.

How do you know if your child has a tongue-tie? One quick way to see is to find out whether your child can poke out his tongue. If his tongue only goes out as far as his lower lip this indicates a tongue-tie. Children with a tongue-tie cannot stretch their tongue right out when licking an ice cream: if you observe them carefully, you will notice they are really using their lips to eat it rather than licking it with their tongue.

There has always been differing opinions regarding whether a tongue-tie should be corrected surgically or not. For many years it was thought that a lot of speech problems were caused by tongue-tie. Even now, we occasionally have a parent come to our clinic saying 'Oh he can't talk properly because he's tongue-tied like his grandfather.' While there may be several members of his family who are tongue-tied, he may have a completely different speech problem. Until recently, speech pathologists thought it was rarely necessary to surgically clip the tongue as children seem to learn to compensate. Surgery does not necessarily alter speech clarity so it is critical to have your speech pathologist do a very thorough oral examination, including observing your child eat and drink, as well as a detailed speech assessment. The latest research, however, indicates that the benefits of surgery (knowing that a child must have a general anaesthetic) are considerable and should be performed as soon as possible. The view is that why should someone have to compensate in the way they eat, drink and speak for the rest of their life when a very quick surgical procedure can eliminate the problem forever? Sometimes it is necessary for the child to have some speech therapy afterwards so they can be taught correct tongue placement for certain speech sounds. Suddenly they have this much more mobile muscle in their mouth and are unsure of where it goes!

Q ARE THE MUSCLES IN MY CHILD'S MOUTH WORKING PROPERLY?

Some children have poor oral coordination and weak muscle control. Look for a child who:

- constantly has his mouth open;
- is constantly dribbling (not only when teething);
- has food falling out of his mouth when eating; or
- is a slow eater, has trouble chewing or regurgitates food down his nose.

All of these signs can be associated with speech problems. For example, when a word combines sounds produced at the back and the front of the mouth ('*kett*le'), one or both of the sounds may be omitted or they may occur in the wrong place. Similarly, words with several syllables ('su-per-mar-ket') may be shortened or mumbled.

Speech pathologists can suggest exercise programs to improve the accuracy and speed of oral muscles. Many children respond well to this therapy and the resulting improvement in speech clarity is obvious.

Some children with poor oral control also have poorer control in other muscles affecting their fine motor skills (for example: threading beads, writing) and even their gross motor skills (for example: running, jumping). In this case an assessment by a paediatrician and occupational therapist would be recommended. Once again, appropriate therapy can improve these skills.

There is also a small group of children who have poor muscle control due to cerebral palsy and Down's syndrome. Because these problems are due to brain damage, either during pregnancy or at birth, it is impossible to 'fix' the muscles and 'cure' the problem. One would aim to achieve the best possible functioning for that child according to their degree of disability.

Q WHEN IS A LISP A PROBLEM?

There are two main types of lisps. The one we are all familiar with is the one demonstrated by cute little three-year-olds whose tongues poke out between their teeth when they say *s* and *z*. This is known as a frontal lisp and should be outgrown by the time a child is five. Unfortunately for many children people just accept that this is the way they speak and do not seek help. You may know of young boys with a lisp who are teased and ridiculed on the football field. How would you feel? We have seen teenage girls who are great at debating or singing but their teachers are leaving them out of events because they lisp. From our point of view, these children need therapy immediately to help them not only correct their lisp but also to improve their self-esteem. Although no-one wants to be teased, sometimes teasing can have a positive impact by motivating the child to succeed in therapy. After five, or if at any time the bite of your child's teeth is affected, then further advice should be sought from a speech pathologist and orthodontist.

The other type of lisp is where the tongue usually cannot be seen but the *s* and *z* sounds are slushy. This is known as a lateral lisp and often your child will be wet and 'splashy' as he speaks. If your child has this type of lisp you should see a speech pathologist, because he will not grow out of this abnormal pattern. The longer it goes on after the age of four-and-a-half, the harder it is to correct the problem. It is important to remember that the motivation of the child and the parents is critical for the intervention to be successful. The child must be willing to practise and you must be willing to set aside the time to help. If not, therapy could be ineffective.

Q I HAVE TO ASK MY CHILD MANY TIMES WHEN I WANT HIM TO DO SOMETHING.
I DON'T BELIEVE HE IS MISBEHAVING BUT I'M SURE HE CAN HEAR.
WHAT'S HAPPENING?

If you have any doubts at all about your child's hearing you should get it tested. Some children are surprisingly clever at picking up clues when they are concentrating but miss clues when their attention is elsewhere. However, if the hearing tests indicate normal hearing it is possible that your child has a problem processing the sounds he hears. This results in what is called a central auditory processing disorder (CAPD). Further investigation is necessary.

Q IS MY CHILD A STUTTERER?

It can be quite a shock for parents when their child wakes one morning and gets stuck on his words: 'I-I-I-I want a drink.' A stutter can appear between the ages of two and seven. A family history of stuttering increases the risk. Numerous repetitions, prolongation of words ('Mmmmummy') and funny faces are also signs of a stutter. If this occurs and you or your child are feeling frustrated, you should seek advice as soon as possible, preferably during the preschool years. Therapy in preschool children can be very effective.

Don't feel anxious about commenting to your child about his stuttering, but do it gently. 'Gut feeling' advice is often appropriate:

'Slow down a bit. Take your time.'

With a child of three or more, you can be more direct:

'You said "Mum" lots of times then. See if you can say it just once. "Mum, can I have a drink please."'

Use slower, steady speech to model for your child.

This is contrary to the more traditional advice to ignore the stutter and just wait patiently for your child to finish. Current research shows beyond question that your child will benefit from your comments. (The approach to an adult with a stutter is very different.)

Children can go through a period of 'normal non-fluency' (or 'developmental stuttering'), especially when their speech and language is expanding quickly and they have a lot to say. They talk like an adult but are not quite ready to do so, resulting in the repetition of a few words. As such, dysfluency refers to a disruption in the rhythm or flow of speech. All of us are dysfluent from time to time and it is accepted as normal because we may just be very tired, under stress or some may have less than adequate motor coordination. If we try to speak very quickly we know that we are more likely to become dysfluent and also 'trip' over words. However, in a child, if dysfluency continues for more than three months, you should consult a speech pathologist. Signs that it may not disappear automatically include a higher frequency of repetitions and prolongation, some 'blocking' whereby the child literally stops mid-sentence and tries to push the word out, an increase in facial grimacing and general frustration and fear of speaking situations.

Q WHAT SHOULD I DO IF MY CHILD CAN'T SAY SOUNDS PROPERLY? IS HE JUST LAZY?

It is unlikely that speech problems are the result of laziness. Most children we know want to be understood and like to be confident in getting their message across. However, sometimes a lack of motivation could be interpreted as laziness. Children who lack motivation may have little confidence and a feeling of hopelessness. They may have never been shown the correct way to make the sounds. Many children, especially school-aged children, are teased because of their speech, language and/or learning problems. When such a child commences therapy we like to think this teasing will have a positive benefit by motivating him to try hard and correct the errors quickly. However, for some children it can have the opposite effect whereby they are simply 'fed up' and can't find the attitude needed to succeed in therapy. They aren't lazy, they have just had enough! If your child has trouble with sounds, try some of the activities suggested in Chapter Three, in the box 'How do we make speech sounds' (pages 50–51). However, if the problems persist, do seek advice from a speech pathologist.

Q SHOULD I WAIT UNTIL MY CHILD STARTS SCHOOL BEFORE DOING ANYTHING ABOUT HIS SPEECH OR LANGUAGE?

No! By the time your child starts school, he should be talking almost as well as you do. Most speech and language problems can be detected before a child starts school so intervention should occur as soon as the problem is identified. If we think of the importance of communication for both academic success and social relationships, then a child who starts kindergarten or school with a speech, language or listening problem will be at a distinct disadvantage immediately.

Whatever the age of your child, if you are anxious, it is better to have your child checked out. Waiting too long may make his problem worse.

Q WHY WILL A SPEECH, LANGUAGE OR LISTENING PROBLEM AFFECT MY CHILD AT SCHOOL?

Let's stop for a moment and think about what happens in a classroom during the day. The teacher does a lot of talking; explains reasons for things occurring, asks questions, gives constant instructions about different activities, tells children what to do for homework and expects the students to remember everything!

So, what skills does a child need if they are to do all of the above? Perhaps most importantly they need to be able to follow the teacher's instructions. To do this, they must have a good knowledge of words and concepts, they must have good hearing and attention skills and their memory must be reasonable. As a child moves through the primary school years, more emphasis is placed on being able to express himself in a clear, coherent fashion. This means he needs to know the rules of grammar, how to construct long and interesting sentences and how to speak clearly so people can understand him. Do you really enjoy listening to a speaker who mumbles, gets lost in his thoughts or repeats himself unnecessarily? We certainly don't!

Literacy (reading, spelling and writing) does not develop easily unless the child has had a solid foundation in speech and language during his preschool years. We need to remember that reading and writing are language skills too, just as talking is. If his speech is unclear or he has specific errors on certain sounds, then it is more likely he will have problems learning to sound out and spell words correctly. If he has a problem with his expressive language such that his verbal language is muddled and incoherent, once he tries to write a story his ideas will become jumbled on paper.

If a child encounters literacy problems in the classroom, he is more at risk of being teased and bullied and the subsequent damage to his self-esteem is often irreversible.

Q I AM FEELING GUILTY ABOUT GOING TO WORK AND LEAVING MY CHILD IN CHILDCARE. WILL IT AFFECT HIS SPEECH AND LANGUAGE DEVELOPMENT?

It is rarely an easy decision to leave your young infant in childcare so you can resume work. Should you also feel guilty and worried that as a result he won't be as good a talker?

There are certainly many factors to consider when choosing childcare, bearing in mind there is never a true replacement for being at home with you! Research has shown that, contrary to what some may think, children who spend time in childcare are not subsequently delayed in speech or language. In fact, they are sometimes more verbal and sociable because they have had to 'fend for themselves' and not rely on you. When our children were toddlers we were very aware of friends' children who were much more confident and socially skilled than ours; theirs went to childcare and ours stayed home with us!

An important consideration when choosing an appropriate place must be the amount of quality language stimulation time each child receives.

If you are considering a childcare centre, visit the centre before making a decision and observe how much time the staff actually spend interacting and talking with each child and what type of interaction is organised. The staff–child ratio will influence this. Many well-meaning centres we have visited have all the right toys and equipment, but at group time the staff seem to spend all their time organising and managing the children which reduces the amount of effective interaction. It is very difficult to engage even a small group of toddlers in an activity and verbally interact well if the teacher is constantly telling children to sit still, not to touch little

Johnny next to them or whatever else. The background educational qualifications of staff are also important. Ensure they have studied early child development and they are organised and confident in their approach. Again, it is useful to spend time observing the staff in action and also chat to parents who already use the facility.

If your child has a speech and/or language difficulty it is wise to ask the speech pathologist to liaise with the childcare centre staff to maximise the child's communication interactions while he is there.

Q WHAT IF MY CHILD HAS TO GO TO HOSPITAL?

For some children a hospital stay may prove to be an important stage in social and emotional development and play a part in the 'growing up' process. On the other hand, a stay in hospital can be traumatic for a toddler and he needs to be well prepared before admission. There are many factors to consider: pain and unpleasantness, parent separation, loneliness, boredom, fear, unfamiliarity and parent anxieties.

Some of the warning signs that the stay in hospital has been traumatic may include regression to more immature behaviours such as thumb-sucking, wanting a dummy and even bed-wetting for the older child. An extended stay may limit the child's contact with peers and may provide little stimulation and opportunity for the child to speak. It is possible that if hospitalisation occurs at a critical time in the child's language development, it may cause a delay. For example, a child may have just started talking at about 14 months and be using several single words when he goes into hospital — he may then stop talking and present six months later with no improvement.

Similar effects on language development may result from other traumatic incidents such as the child's mother or father going away for a few weeks or a new baby coming into the family.

Q WILL MY CHILD'S SPEECH AND LANGUAGE DEVELOPMENT BE AFFECTED BY WHETHER THEY ARE A GIRL OR A BOY?

Despite the many factors contributing to a child's rate of speech and language development, you often hear people say 'Boys are slower than girls.' Could this be true?

Studies of young girls and boys have shown there to be no significant difference on language test scores, implying they both develop language at the same rate. What has been shown however, is that different aspects of language seem to be acquired at different times during the preschool years. Girls tend to use 'emotion' words before boys, while boys tend to use more 'action' words earlier on. Girls will usually use language to interact with peers and solve problems at an earlier age, they will initiate more conversation and talk through their problems; whereas boys will typically solve problems through actions. Most of us would agree this difference also exists between adult males and females. I'm sure many women have heard their partners say 'You always want to talk about things'! Both young boys and young girls are equally successful at solving problems; they just do it differently.

Research into the way parents interact with their two- and three-year-olds has shown that different language styles are used with boys and girls. Maybe we are partly responsible for the differences between our sons and daughters! Studies have shown that 78 per cent of young girls used a more expressive style of language, that is, they used more nouns (names of objects), preferred naming games and had clearer speech; whereas only 60 per cent of the boys demonstrated this style of language at the same age. Mothers of two-year-old girls talked more during their play interactions and also during non-play situations. They asked more open-ended questions and talked more with their daughters when help was needed. In contrast, mothers of two-year-old boys initiated conversation with them more often in play situations but not in non-play situations. When their mothers played with them, boys tended to use less complex language, referring more to the present and to the actions rather than naming items. Observations of toddlers' play showed that the boys playing with vehicles used more sounds and noises rather than real words while the girls playing with dolls used more naming words. It is therefore a good idea to move away from these stereotyped play situations and allow your daughters to play with 'boys' toys' and vice versa.

Q WILL MY CHILD BE A FAST OR SLOW TALKER
ACCORDING TO HIS BIRTH ORDER?

As is the case with gender differences, there is no real disadvantage in being the first- or last-born and there is no evidence to suggest that birth order is linked to language learning problems.

Studies have shown that while the first-born has a larger vocabulary during his second year of life, siblings learn language in the same way. The differences tend to occur because of the very nature of differences in the second child's and subsequent children's language environment. We would all agree that our first child had more individual time with us and therefore received much more direct language modelling. Even we feel guilty! However, a second child has the benefit of sibling interaction. Research has shown that second children have better conversational skills at an earlier age, they have more idea of turn-taking in conversations, they stay on topic more often and they use more pronouns ('he', 'she', 'they') at an earlier age than their first-born sibling. Maybe this is linked to the fact that second-born children develop friendships earlier on. Why this happens is unclear but, if we think of mealtime situations in our own houses, then our second-born was exposed to more socially complex conversations at an earlier age. There are more people interacting and talking!

How often have we heard it said 'Oh he's just slow to talk because the older kids talk for him.' Well, this could be the case but we should never assume that the child who isn't talking, or is delayed, could talk if the others didn't talk for him. We would advise you to seek help in spite of this. Parents need to know that even if the older child talks for the younger child, we should still expect the younger one to talk.

Q IS MY CHILD 'BACKWARDS' BECAUSE HE HAS SPEECH PROBLEMS?

Children who are intellectually disabled frequently have unclear speech. However, if your child has a specific speech and/or language problem it does *not* mean he is intellectually disabled. Even gifted and talented children can have speech difficulties.

A speech pathologist will assess all aspects of your child's speech and language development. She will also ask you information about early progress in other areas of development. This would include factors relating to feeding as a baby, as well as physical development and play skills.

It is true to say that the earlier your child can develop his communication skills the more he reduces the chances of having difficulties with reading and writing.

Q MY CHILD'S SPEECH PATHOLOGIST HAS SAID I NEED TO TAKE HIM TO A PSYCHOLOGIST FOR AN INTELLECTUAL ASSESSMENT. WHAT DOES THIS MEAN? WHAT DOES THIS HAVE TO DO WITH HIS LANGUAGE PROBLEM?

Many children we see for therapy do benefit from having an assessment by a qualified psychologist. Many people baulk when they hear the word 'psychologist' because it seems to imply that their personal life is going to be 'analysed'! This is not typically the reason why your speech pathologist would want to refer your child. Her reason would most likely be for your child to have an intellectual assessment, otherwise known as an IQ test.

What's involved in having an IQ test? Firstly, try to think of us as having two lots of intelligence — a nonverbal one and a verbal one. Each of these has its place in helping us to learn different tasks. Nonverbal tasks mean that we don't rely on the spoken word to complete the task, for example, we can do a puzzle or a maze without having to speak. Verbal tasks do rely on the spoken word, for example, 'Tell me the names of as many zoo animals as you can think of.' Therefore, each of these tasks requires a different part of our brain (or intelligence) to be working. When a psychologist gives an IQ test, the child is presented with a series of problem-solving tasks and their ability to observe, reason and carry out the task is evaluated. For the nonverbal tasks, equipment such as blocks, puzzles and pictures are used, and for the verbal tasks questions may be asked.

What does this testing have to do with your child's language problem? Well, it would most likely be suggested for children who are having difficulties with their understanding of language. If your child cannot follow verbal instructions it is important to ensure it is an isolated language problem and not due to a broader intellectual problem. This is critical to an accurate diagnosis and to determine the most appropriate method of management. The testing will highlight the child's strengths and weaknesses which are again important for the planning of therapy. We all know that we can effectively use our strength areas to maximise learning in our weaker areas. In relation to a child who has difficulty following verbal instructions, he can be greatly assisted if visual cues are provided as well. For example, if you said, 'Put the cup on the table' he might not understand the words and therefore not do it. However, if you said, 'Put the cup on the table' and as you said it you held up a picture of a cup and a table, he would be more likely to do it. You could also demonstrate the action of doing it for him. By seeing you do it or by seeing the pictures, he is using his stronger visual skills to help him complete a verbal task which he finds difficult.

Another aspect of a psychologist's testing may be to seek information from you about your child's behaviour and home routines. It is not a way of examining your parenting skills, but rather a way of assisting in making the correct diagnosis and formulating subsequent management strategies. Sometimes a child's behaviour can get in the way of his progress, particularly if he is frustrated by his language problems.

Q MY CHILD'S SPEECH PATHOLOGIST HAS SUGGESTED I HAVE HIM ASSESSED BY AN OCCUPATIONAL THERAPIST.
WHAT DOES THIS MEAN?
WHAT DOES THIS HAVE TO DO WITH HIS SPEECH PROBLEM?

In its broadest sense, an occupational therapist (or OT) is someone who is involved with people 'doing and achieving within their occupations'. In relation to children, they help them 'cope' with many areas of daily living whether at home or at school. There is, at times, a close relationship between a child's language difficulties and other more physical-type skills and hence an overlap may exist in the intervention process. Research by an American OT, Jean Ayres, in the 1960s discovered that a group of language-impaired children also had difficulties in the areas of fine motor and writing skills, visual perceptual skills, establishing a dominance for handedness, self-care skills and attention and physical restlessness. If you relate some of the characteristics we've discussed in relation to speech and language problems to these areas of difficulty found by Jean Ayres, then you can see why your speech pathologist might like your child to see an occupational therapist.

The common connections between the two areas are illustrated by the following examples. Young children with speech problems such as dyspraxia sometimes have problems with oral and overall body sensitivity. The dyspraxic child's inability to produce movements on command may mean he has problems with self-feeding, dressing and writing skills. Children with language difficulties often display poor attention and poor organisational skills. If they have problems sequencing words in the right order, they may also have problems sequencing movements of their body and being aware of where their body is in space. Such children are often described as 'clumsy', 'messy', 'sloppy', 'fidgety' and 'restless'.

An assessment by an OT would involve looking at your child's ability to manage with dressing, eating, bathing, etc. according to what is age-appropriate. They would assess eye–hand coordination, visual motor abilities, body awareness, coordination of body movements, hand preference as well as many other related areas. Can your child do puzzles and thread beads? Does he keep dropping the beads as he tries to thread them? Does he often bump into furniture or other people? Does he slouch all over the desk and find it tiring to sit up straight? If there are problems in these areas then it may well be that intervention will also assist progress in speech- or language-related areas. He may be able to listen more easily because he can sit up straight for a longer period of time. He may be less frustrated when writing stories because he has learnt the hand control and correct pencil grip necessary to make writing easier.

Different therapy approaches exist and hopefully, like your speech pathologist, the OT will take an eclectic approach using a variety of treatment techniques appropriate to your child's individual needs. One treatment approach does not suit every type of problem!

Sensory integration is one approach to managing some 'OT problems'. Sensory integration techniques involve the child in movement, swinging, spinning and attaining balance. The theory is that these actions help brain maturation, which subsequently leads to improved academic and other abilities. Research and anecdotal evidence vary as to the benefits of this approach and, like any other professional visit with your child, you have the right to ask questions and observe what happens in therapy.

12 Developmental milestones

We have put together a list of the developmental milestones for the first five years of life. Of course children progress and reach these milestones at different ages and stages. Those listed here aim to provide you with guidelines for reference on communication, language, social and motor skills by the time your child reaches these ages. Do remember that development is frequently uneven. Generally though large motor movements will precede fine motor movements and understanding of language will precede talking.

If at any stage you have any queries or concerns we encourage you to seek professional guidance and advice.

0–3 Months

Understanding
- responds to sound — some loud noises may still cause distress
- recognises familiar voices around him
- gazes at a speaker's face
- looks at a clear, simple picture
- recognises familiar routines, e.g. feeding. He might even start anticipating routines

Motor skills
- sucks and swallows, which is essential for feeding and the development of facial muscles
- sleeps for a great deal of the time when not being fed
- moves less jerkily
- kicks legs vigorously

Communication
- cries when hungry. He is yet to learn to wait
- gurgles and makes vowel-like sounds especially in response to your sounds
- smiles

Social skills
- is unpredictable
- enjoys being cuddled and spoken to
- lifts head to look around
- feels, tastes, smells and hears

4–6 Months

Understanding
- turns his head to find the source of the sound that catches his attention
- is startled by loud noises
- recognises own name when called
- recognises names of familiar people, e.g. Mummy, Daddy
- recognises the difference between angry and friendly voices

Motor skills
- looks at hands and feet and plays with both
- supports head and chest with arms when on stomach
- tries to roll over
- sits with or without support
- holds something in either hand to look at it
- bounces when held in standing position
- explores objects with his mouth

Communication
- makes sounds in response to speech
- makes a variety of speech sounds
- uses different cries to mean different things
- laughs and chuckles in play
- screams with annoyance
- shakes rattle deliberately to make a sound

Social skills
- enjoys looking in the mirror
- recognises familiar situations, e.g. bath time
- enjoys playing peek-a-boo
- purposely drops object to have it returned to him. He will continue this game long after you have had enough
- is friendly with strangers

7–9 Months

Understanding
- understands the word 'no', especially when a firm tone of voice is used
- recognises common objects by name, especially items he is particularly fond of or uses frequently
- enjoys noise-making toys
- looks at pictures when named

Motor skills
- picks up cup/finger food etc.
- feeds himself with finger foods. This may be messy but enjoyable for him
- pulls himself up to standing position
- is mobile. He will suddenly seem to be everywhere at once and you need to keep a close watch on where he is
- picks up small objects and puts them into his mouth. As he is mobile be careful what he finds to place in his mouth
- picks up, pushes and shoves large things

Communication
- copies speech sounds
- uses a greater variety of sounds. These are becoming identifiable with the language he is learning
- makes noise with things on purpose
- uses simple gestures, e.g. waves bye-bye, claps
- shouts to attract attention

Social skills
- plays an increasing variety of games, e.g. pat-a-cake
- shows anxiety when a familiar person leaves the room
- distinguishes strangers from familiar faces
- manipulates objects with interest, passing them from hand to hand
- looks for a toy falling over the edge of a pram or table
- watches movements of other people

10–12 Months

Understanding
- responds well to his name
- responds to familiar sounds, e.g. phone ringing
- follows simple commands

Motor skills
- sits on a chair
- drops things into a small opening
- crawls, scoots, creeps or walks from one place to another
- points with index finger at objects he wants or which interests him
- uses both hands freely (but he may show a preference for one)

Communication
- responds by nodding or shaking his head
- uses increasing amount of speech, which may sound as if he is talking
- varies pitch and loudness of sounds
- names familiar objects/people
- indicates his basic wants, e.g. biscuit, juice

Social skills
- plays simple make-believe games
- uses gestures, e.g. waving
- helps with dressing
- repeats activities to reproduce effects, e.g. throws objects deliberately onto the floor
- likes to be constantly within sight and hearing of adults
- looks in the correct place for toys which have rolled out of sight

13–18 Months

Understanding
- shakes his head appropriately for simple yes/no questions
- moves rhythmically to music
- enjoys simple rhymes and songs
- understands many words and simple directions
- shows at least one body part

Motor skills
- walks well
- starts and stops safely
- picks up a toy from the floor without falling
- spontaneously scribbles when given a crayon
- turns two or three pages at a time
- picks up small beads etc. with delicate first finger and thumb movement
- pushes, pulls or carries toy while walking
- uses a spoon to scoop
- uses toys without taking them to his mouth

Communication
- jabbers tunefully to himself
- uses some words correctly
- attempts to sing
- demands desired objects by pointing and talking/grunting
- echoes the prominent or last word said to him
- initiates simple activities, e.g. sweeping the floor or reading

Social skills
- explores the environment energetically
- remembers where objects belong
- plays alone contentedly but likes to be near an adult
- still is emotionally dependent on a familiar adult
- alternates between clinging and resistance
- enjoys doing the same things over and over again

2 Years

Understanding
- points to five body parts
- listens to a short story
- matches sounds to animals
- recognises pictures and names them

Motor skills
- throws a ball
- strings large beads
- runs fast
- turns one page at a time
- tries to jump
- chews food well
- tries to balance on one foot
- turns door handles

Communication
- uses his own name
- says two-word sentences, e.g. 'more milk'
- uses words that tell what people or things do
- uses words that tell about people and things
- sings some words to songs
- uses many but not all sounds accurately
- uses 50 or more words
- talks continually while playing
- constantly asks for names of objects

Social skills
- shows emotions
- copies housework
- feels frustrated easily
- tries to comfort others
- follows Mummy or Daddy around the house copying domestic activities
- constantly demands Mummy's or Daddy's attention
- has tantrums when frustrated
- has no idea of sharing
- plays near other children but not with them

2½ Years

Understanding
- enjoys familiar stories
- selects correct items from a choice of five upon request
- understands many complex sentences

Motor skills
- jumps with two feet together
- sits on a tricycle and propels himself with feet on the ground
- builds a tower of seven blocks
- eats skilfully with a spoon and fork
- walks upstairs alone
- kicks a large ball
- pushes and pulls toys skilfully

Communication
- says his full name
- talks intelligibly to himself at play concerning events happening here and now
- uses 200 or more recognisable words
- continually asks *what* and *where* questions
- uses pronouns 'I', 'me' and 'we'
- has the beginnings of a crude grammar, e.g. 'I goed'
- no longer is using jargon
- has speech that might be non-fluent (similar to stuttering) in his eagerness to talk

Social skills
- is often very active and restless
- engages in prolonged domestic make-believe play, e.g. putting dolls to bed
- watches other children at play and occasionally joins in for a few minutes
- has very little idea about sharing toys or adults' attention

3 Years

Understanding
- listens eagerly to new stories
- seems to understand most of what is being said to him
- begins to identify objects by use, e.g. 'What do we eat with?'
- chooses between objects
- shows an understanding of past and present
- knows several nursery rhymes
- understands about 1000 words

Motor skills
- climbs nursery equipment with agility
- turns around obstacles and corners when running
- stands momentarily on one foot
- walks on tiptoe
- copies a circle
- starts cutting with scissors

Communication
- talks in short sentences
- uses a large vocabulary
- asks many *what*, *where* and *who* questions
- speaks more clearly but still has many errors
- names one colour
- uses speech that may often have repetitions of words, especially when excited or anxious
- uses plurals, e.g. 'dogs'
- uses past tense, e.g. 'jumped'
- initiates a conversation
- carries on a simple conversation
- is understood most of the time within the family

Social skills
- has general behaviour that's more amenable
- enjoys dramatic make-believe play including pretend objects and people
- joins in play with other children inside and outdoors
- understands sharing, although won't always do so
- shows affection for younger siblings
- does easy picture matching

4 Years

Understanding
- locates the source of sound
- knows several colours
- puts simple objects into groups, e.g. foods
- understands some opposites
- understands past, present and future

Motor skills
- climbs ladders and trees
- is an expert rider of a tricycle
- does a five- to ten-piece puzzle
- screws a lid onto a jar
- does simple block-building
- matches a simple bead or block design
- draws a basic picture of a man
- hops on one foot
- dresses and undresses himself except for laces and back buttons
- catches a bean bag in one hand

Communication
- uses speech that is completely intelligible, with few sound substitutions remaining
- gives a connected account of recent events and experiences
- recites a rhyme or song
- explains what an item is used for, e.g. 'cup is for drinking'
- uses pronouns, e.g. 'he', 'she'
- uses possessive pronouns, e.g. 'his', 'hers'
- uses sentences that are grammatically correct most of the time
- constantly asks *why* and *how* questions
- asks what words mean
- listens to and tells long stories, sometimes confusing fact and fantasy

Social skills
- takes part in a short group-time
- talks to friends while playing
- has general behaviour that is self-willed
- is inclined to verbal impertinence but can be affectionate and compliant
- needs other children to play with and is alternatively cooperative and aggressive with them and with adults
- understands turn-taking
- shows concern for younger siblings and sympathy for playmates in distress

5 Years

Understanding
- appreciates the meaning of clock time in relation to the daily program
- understands most of what is heard
- understands right and left
- appreciates humour

Motor skills
- runs lightly on toes
- skips on alternate feet
- writes a few letters
- draws a recognisable man
- is skilful in climbing, sliding and swinging
- uses a knife and fork

Communication
- speaks in complete sentences
- uses speech that is fluent and grammatical
- has articulation that is correct except for residual confusions in s/f/th and r/l/w/y groups, therefore speech is clear most of the time
- explains what you can do with things
- makes up stories and provides a lot of information
- asks the meaning of abstract words
- gives details of his address
- uses past, present and future tenses
- has a large and varied vocabulary of 2000 words or more
- asks quite complex questions, e.g. 'Why did that happen?'

Social skills
- general behaviour is more sensible, controlled and responsibly independent
- plays complicated floor games
- chooses own friends
- is cooperative with companions and understands the need for rules and fair play
- is protective towards other children
- continues a game from one day to another
- maintains attention for conversation, movies etc.
- works independently
- counts up to 30 in a sequence
- participates in class discussions

Glossary

age equivalent (AE) A score used in a report to indicate how a child's performance compares to normal developing children. It is represented in years and months. For example, if a child obtains an age-equivalent score of 4–7 on a test, this means he performed as you would expect a 'typical' child of four years seven months to perform.

ankyloglossia Another name for tongue-tie. The tissue connecting the tongue (frenum) to the bottom of the mouth is too short or, in other words, the tissue under the tongue is too close to the tongue tip. This results in restricted mobility during talking and swallowing.

apraxia (or dyspraxia) Difficulty in planning and initiating movements when required, i.e. on command.

articulation The way we produce or pronounce speech sounds.

Asperger's syndrome One of the autism spectrum disorders characterised by difficulties in social interaction, including poor use of language for social interaction.

attention deficit hyperactivity disorder (ADHD) A syndrome characterised by some combination of problems in sustaining attention, impulse control and overactivity.

audiogram A drawn diagram representing the results of a hearing test.

audiologist A specialist trained to perform hearing tests.

auditory (or verbal) comprehension The ability to understand the spoken word.

auditory discrimination The ability to hear the differences in sounds.

auditory memory The ability to remember information that was heard and not seen.

auditory processing The ability to sort out and make sense of sounds heard.

autism A severe developmental disorder characterised by impaired social interaction and communication skills. The processing and use of sensory information is also impaired.

babbling The sounds a baby makes when he combines a consonant and vowel sound and then repeats this syllable combination over and over.

central auditory processing disorder A disorder characterised by difficulty in attending to or processing speech in distracting listening environments.

cerebral palsy A condition caused by brain damage resulting in a disorder of movement and posture. The brain damage usually occurs before, during or just after birth.

chronological age (or CA) The child's age in years and months as listed on reports, e.g. 3–6 yrs means three years and six months old.

cleft palate A congenital fissure (or opening) of the soft palate and roof of the mouth. It sometimes extends through the upper lip.

cluttering Very rapid nervous speech characterised by the omission of sounds or syllables.

code switching A conscious or purposeful switching of two languages within one sentence or between sentences, as seen in bilingual speakers.

cognitive development The process by which a child comes to make sense of the world. It involves what he sees, hears, touches, smells and feels.

communication The exchanging of information, ideas and feelings using speech, symbols or writing.

consonant A letter whose sound is made by partially or completely blocking the breath stream. There are 21 consonants in the English language, such as *b, k, r, s.*

decibel A unit for measuring the intensity of sound.

developmental delay When a child's skills are developing significantly slower than children of his age. This can occur in cognitive, language, physical, or social/emotional development.

developmental dyspraxia The form of apraxia seen in children as opposed to an acquired dyspraxia more often seen in adults after a stroke. Children with dyspraxia have difficulty organising and sequencing the motor movement necessary for speech.

Down's syndrome A genetic condition caused by a chromosome abnormality. These children have a set of common features different from others with an intellectual disability.

dysarthria A disorder of articulation due to impairment of the part of the central nervous system which directly controls speech muscles.

dysfluency Another term for stuttering.

echolalia A pattern of responding by repeating all or part of what was heard. It is most commonly associated with children who have poor understanding of language.

ENT ear, nose and throat, as in an ENT specialist.

eustachian tube A tube that connects the middle ear to the throat and whose function it is to equalise the air pressure between the two sides of the eardrum.

expansion A technique used to encourage more language by repeating what your child says and also adding a few more words.

expressive language The transforming of our ideas into the spoken or written word.

expressive vocabulary The repertoire of words we use when speaking.

fluency The ability to speak in a smooth natural flow.

formal tests (or standardised tests) Commercially available tests which provide statistical information about a child's performance in comparison to what is expected for an 'average' child of that age. Statistics used in reports include age-equivalent scores, percentile ranks and standard scores.

grammar The rules of a language that determine how we form and order words to construct a sentence.

hearing The physical ability to respond to a sound.

informal tests Often considered a less threatening way of examining a child's skills than administering formal tests. Informal testing is done by way of observing the child in a variety of activities and situations, such as playing with toys or responding to questions in a relaxed conversational situation.

intelligence quotient (IQ) A measurement of our ability to understand, learn and solve problems quickly.

intonation The 'music' or sound patterns we produce by varying our voice. Also known as inflection.

jargon The early language sounds an infant makes by joining sounds together and using real inflection in the voice. Unlike babbling, which is a repetition of the same sound combination in each syllable, jargon contains different sound combinations in each syllable.

language The set of symbols used by a group of people to communicate. It can be in the form of gestural, spoken or written symbols.

language development The way a child learns to understand what is happening and how to express his thoughts.

language delay A child's language is following the normal pathways of development but at a slower rate.

language disorder A child's language is significantly impaired in understanding and/or expression and it is not following the normal pattern of development.

lisp A speech problem characterised by a distortion of the sounds 's' and 'z'. The most common form of lisp is where the child's tongue protrudes between the teeth as he says these sounds.

listening The way we pay attention to the sounds we hear so we can interpret their meaning.

literacy The ability to use language by reading and writing.

long-term memory our permanent memory storehouse of information.

modelling Providing examples of correct speech or language responses to stimulate the child to use them himself.

morphology The sounds or syllables on the beginning or end of a word that indicate its meaning. An example is the 's' on the end of a word, such as 'bed', which shows us there is more than one bed, so the 's' is known as a plural morpheme.

multisyllable word A word which contains more than one syllable or part. For example, 'book' has one syllable and 'ra-bbit' has two syllables. Multisyllable words are often used in therapy to improve a child's speech clarity.

normal non-fluency A period of dysfluent speech common in preschoolers and characterised by the repetition of some words. It usually only lasts a few months.

normal development The level of skill considered by experts to be typical for a certain age.

oral-motor skills The ability to perform certain movements with the muscles of the mouth area including the tongue, lips and cheeks.

otitis media A middle-ear infection, usually with fluid present behind the eardrum.

overbite The extent to which the upper front teeth overlap the lower teeth.

paediatrician A doctor who specialises in children's diseases.

parallel talk A technique designed to stimulate language. It is the way we talk out loud or give a running commentary about what our child is doing at the time.

percentile (PR or Percentile Rank) The number that compares a person's score on a formal test to others of the same age. For example, a child receiving a percentile score of 15 means that for every 100 children, he does better than 15 of them.

pervasive developmental disorder (PDD) A neurological disorder similar to autism. Children are sometimes diagnosed with PDD when they display similar behaviours but do not meet the criteria for autism disorder.

phonics Associating a sound with a single letter or combination of letters.

phonological awareness A set of skills known to be essential if the child is to become a competent reader. Also known as sound awareness. It includes the skills of word and sound awareness, the recognition and production of syllables, sounds and rhyme, and the ability to blend sounds together to form a word.

phonological disorder A significant speech difficulty characterised by problems in understanding the rules of how sounds are used in speech. It results in multiple speech sound errors and poor clarity.

pragmatics How language is used in social situations.

prognosis A prediction of the outcome of a problem.

raw score The number of points scored on a test. This number is then converted to a standard deviation.

receptive language The language that we understand or comprehend. The term is synonymous with language comprehension.

receptive vocabulary The words a person can understand, that is, the extent of his word knowledge.

self-talk Refers to you talking out loud about what you are doing at that particular time, unlike parallel talk, which is the talking out loud that you do about what your child is doing at that time. It is a technique used to stimulate early language.

semantics The vocabulary we use to convey our meaning.

semantic pragmatic disorder This is characterised by a good vocabulary but poor use of it. Poor knowledge of the rules of language in social interaction.

sequencing Putting things in the correct order. It could be related to the sequencing of sounds, words or pictures.

short-term memory Our temporary working memory.

speech The sounds we make to communicate a message verbally.

speech pathologist (or speech therapist) A specialist trained to diagnose and treat problems of speech, language and listening in children and adults. The term varies within and between countries.

standard score (SS) A score based on a system whereby 100 or sometimes 10 is average. The average range also varies from test to test. Usually 80 and 120 (8 or 12) is considered an average range. Scores below 80 or 8 might be investigated further.

stuttering A disturbance of the rhythm and fluency of speech, characterised by blocking, repetition or prolongation of sounds and words.

syllable A part of a word which is pronounced as a unit or segment. It contains a single vowel sound and may or may not contain a consonant sound. For example, 'su-per-mar-ket' has four syllables.

syntax The grammatical arrangement of words to form sentences.

tongue-thrust Occurs when the tongue pushes forward between the teeth instead of moving backwards when swallowing. It can lead to dental and speech problems.

vocabulary The words of a language.

vowel A speech sound made with the mouth open and the stream of breath unobstructed by the tongue, teeth or lips. The English language has five vowel sounds, *a*, *e*, *i*, *o* and *u*.

word-finding problem (or word-retrieval problem) A difficulty in thinking of a familiar word when required.

Children's booklist

Here is a recommended reading list of books to help promote your child's language development. You may find many of them at your local library. Remember, too, that books make excellent presents.

Nursery rhymes and rhythmical books

These are often the first books that we read to young infants. They are fun, bouncy and good for getting both you and your child to look at and play with each other. You will be surprised how quickly your child seems to remember the words and actions of the rhymes.

Brown, Mark Tolon, 1994, *Party Rhymes*, Picture Puffins, UK.

Chamberlain, Margaret, 1994, *abc rhymes*, Ladybird, UK.

Gardner, Sally, 1996, *Playtime Rhymes*, Orion Publishing Group, London, UK.

Lewis, Stephen, 2000, *Action Rhymes for You and Your Friends*, Dorling Kindersley, Australia.

Ormerod, Jan, 1988, *Rhymes Around the Day*, Picture Puffins, London, UK.
Wadsworth, Olive, 1971, *Over in the Meadow*, Four Winds Press, New Zealand.
Hill, Eric, 1996, *Fairy Tales: A Lift the Flap Book*, Puffin Books, Australia.

Repetitive stories

A child is never too young to have these books read to them. Like nursery rhymes, these books will be remembered easily because of the repetitive nature of the words throughout the story.

Alborough, Jez, 1993, *Washing Line*, Walker Books, London, UK.
Allen, Pamela, 1984, *Bertie and the Bear*, Berkley Publishing Group, USA.
Allen, Pamela, 1988, *Who Sank the Boat?*, Puffin Books, Australia.
Asch, Frank, 2000, *Just Like Daddy*, Carousel Books, USA.
Campbell, Rod, 1986, *Oh Dear!*, Simon & Schuster, London, UK.
Crebbin, June, 1995, *The Train Ride*, Walker Books, London, UK.
Dale, Penny, 1988, *Ten in the Bed*, William Heinemann, Australia.
Fox, Mem, 1993, *Time for Bed*, Omnibus Books, South Australia.
Gale, Leah, 1987, *The Animals of Farmer Jones*, Golden Books, USA.
Kalan, Robert, 1989, *Jump, Frog, Jump*, Mulberry Books, Canada.
Kerr, Judith, 1991, *Mog and the Baby*, HarperCollins*Publishers*, Australia.
Kerr, Judith, 1994, *Mog in the Garden*, HarperCollins*Publishers*, Australia.
Kerr, Judith, 2003, *Mog's Kittens*, HarperCollins*Publishers*, Australia.
Lacome, Julie, 1993, *Walking Through the Jungle*, Walker Books, London, UK.
Maris, Ron, 1986, *Are You There, Bear?*, Picture Puffin, Australia.
Maris, Ron, 1982, *Better Move On, Frog*, Grolier Publishing, USA.
Martin, Bill Jr, 1995, *Brown Bear, Brown Bear*, Puffin Books, London, UK.

Simple stories

There are so many books we could include in this section. Here are a few which have been favourites of our children from when they were infants until even now, when they will be taken from the bookcase to read silently or have us read aloud to them. All of these titles are readily available at libraries and booksellers everywhere.

Ahlberg, Janet & Allan, 1978, *Each Peach Pear Plum*, Puffin Books, London, UK.
Ahlberg, Janet, 1990, *Starting School*, Picture Puffins, London, UK.
Alborough, Jez, 2002, *Captain Duck*, HarperCollins*Publishers*, Australia.
Alborough, Jez, 2002, *Fix It Duck*, HarperCollins*Publishers*, Australia.
Allen, Pamela, 1998, *Alexander's Outing*, Puffin Books, London, UK.
Allen, Pamela, 1998, *Belinda*, Puffin Books, London, UK.
Allen, Pamela, 1980, *Mr Archimedes' Bath*, William Morrow & Company, New York, USA.

Campbell, Rod, 1998, *Dear Zoo*, Puffin Books, London, UK.

Carle, Eric, 1988, *The Very Busy Spider*, Hamish Hamilton, London, UK.

Carle, Eric, 1997, *The Very Hungry Caterpillar*, Picture Puffin, Australia.

Churchill, Vicki, 2001, *Sometimes I Like To Curl Up in a Ball*, Gullane Children's Books, London, UK.

Cousins, Lucy, 1995, *Za-Za's Baby Brother*, Walker Books, London, UK.

Dodd, Lynley, 1984, *Hairy Maclary's Bone*, Mallinson Rendel, New Zealand.

Dodd, Lynley, 1985, *Hairy Maclary Scattercat*, Puffin Books, Australia.

Eastman, P.D., 2003, *Big Dog, Little Dog*, Random House, Australia.

Edwards, Hazel, 1989, *My Hippopotamus is On Our Caravan Roof Getting Sunburnt*, Hodder & Stoughton, Australia.

Edwards, Hazel, 1980, *There's a Hippopotamus On Our Roof Eating Cake*, Hodder & Stoughton, Australia.

Graham, Amanda, 1985, *Picasso the Green Tree Frog*, Era Publications, USA.

Gunson, Jonathan, 1985, *Mr Smudge's Thirsty Day*, Reed Methuen, New Zealand.

Hughes, Shirley, 1988, *Sally's Secret*, Viking Press, New York, USA.

Hutchins, Pat, *Rosie's Walk*, Picture Puffin, UK.

Kerr, Judith, 1993, *The Tiger Who Came to Tea*, HarperCollins Juvenile Books, USA.

McBratney, Sam, 1994, *Guess How Much I Love You*, Walker Books, London, UK.

McDonnell, Flora, 1995, *I Love Boats*, Walker Books, London, UK.

Murphy, Jill, 1986, *Five Minutes' Peace*, Walker Books, London, UK.

Pank, Rachel, 1996, *Little Big Sister*, HarperCollins*Publishers*, Australia.

Rubenstein, Gillian, 1992, *Dog In, Cat Out*, Scholastic, Australia.

Wells, Rosemary, 1997, *Noisy Nora*, Picture Puffin, Australia.

Winer, Yvonne, 1985, *Mr Brown's Magnificent Apple Tree*, Scholastic, Australia.

More complex stories and picture books for older children

These books are also very popular and readily available. The text in this selection is less repetitive and contains more complex vocabulary.

Ahlberg, Janet & Allan, 1977, *Burglar Bill*, William Morrow & Company, New York, USA.

Ahlberg, Janet & Allan, 1986, *The Jolly Postman*, Puffin Books, London, UK.

Andreae, Giles, 1999, *Giraffes Can't Dance*, Orchard Books, London, UK.

Anholt, Catherine & Laurence, 1998, *Big Book of Families*, Walker Books, London. UK.

Baker, Jeannie, 1994, *Grandmother*, Ashton Scholastic, Australia.

Baker, Jeannie, 1987, *Where the Forest Meets the Sea*, Walker Books, London, UK.

Barber, Shirley, 1993, *The Enchanted Woods*, Five Mile Press, Australia.

Bemelmans, Ludwig, 1962, *Madeline in London*, Scholastic Children's Books, London, UK.

Carle, Eric, 1977, *The Bad Tempered Ladybird*, Penguin Books, London, UK.

Egan, Cecilia, 1999, *The Frog Who Wouldn't Laugh*, JB Books, South Australia.

Hoban, Russell, 1994, *A Birthday for Frances*, HarperCollins*Publishers*, Australia.

Hoban, Russell, 1993, *Bread and Jam for Frances*, HarperCollins*Publishers*, Australia.

Langen, Annette, 1994, *Letters From Felix*, Moondrake, Australia.

Lester, Alison, 1989, *Imagine*, Allen & Unwin, Australia.

Northeast, Brenda, 1997, *For the Love of Auguste*, Mammoth, Australia.

Pfister, Marcus, 1998, *Rainbow Fish and the Big Blue Whale*, North-South Books, New York, USA.

Piers, Helen, 1982, *Long Neck and Thunder Foot*, Picture Puffin, UK.

Rayner, Mary, 1980, *The Rain Cloud*, Atheneum, USA.

Sheldon, Dyan, 1990, *The Whales' Song*, Random House, UK.

Viorst, Judith, 1976, *Alexander and the Terrible, Horrible, No Good, Very Bad Day*, Simon&Schuster, Australia.

Wells, Rosemary, 2000, *Timothy Goes to School*, Picture Puffin, UK.

Rhyming and poetry books

These books are more focussed on teaching children the important skills of rhyming, alliteration and word manipulation which are necessary for reading and spelling. They introduce poetry and humorous verse.

Ireson, Barbara, 1971, *The Young Puffin Book of Verse*, Penguin Putnam, New York, USA.

Levine, Caroline Anne, 1985, *Knockout Knock Knocks*, Penguin Putnam, Australia.

Parish, Peggy, 1992, *Amelia Bedelia*, HarperCollins*Publishers*, Australia.

Parish, Peggy, 1997, *Amelia Bedelia Helps Out*, HarperCollins*Publishers*, Australia.

Terban, Marvin, 1982, *Eight Ate: A Feast of Homonym Riddles*, Houghton Mifflin, USA.

Webb, Kaye, 1999, *I Like This Poem*, Penguin, UK.

Early readers

There are numerous reader series available today. Your child's preschool or school will certainly be able to offer suggestions beyond what your child brings home as his reader. Here are a few examples of early readers and chapter books.

Barry, Margaret, 1994, *Simon and the Witch*, Fontana Collins, London, UK.

Barry, Margaret, 1997, *The Return of the Witch*, Fontana Collins, London, UK.

Cameron, Ann, 1989, *Stories Julian Tells*, Random House London, UK.

Clark, Margaret, 1999, *Hello, Possum*, Hodder Headline, Australia.

Cleary, Beverly, 1995, *Ramona the Brave*, Camelot Publishers, USA.

Cleary, Beverly, 1996, *Ramona the Pest*, Puffin Books, London, UK.

Cooling, Wendy, 1996, *Stories for Five-Year-Olds and Other Young Readers*, Puffin
    Books, London, UK.
Storr, Catherine, 1992, *Clever Polly and the Stupid Wolf*, Young Puffin, London, UK.
Storr, Catherine, 1993, *Polly and the Wolf Again*, Young Puffin, London, UK.

Popular reader series used in schools:
Aussie Nibbles
Aussie Bites
Read with Ladybird
Tadpole

Books for more advanced readers

Levels of reading ability vary enormously in our population. Within any primary
school classroom there will be significant differences in reading levels. Make your
own judgment about a book's suitability based on your own knowledge of your
child's ability, rather than age guidelines. Remember too, as parents, you can read
aloud novels that may be too advanced for your child to read alone but he will still
learn a lot from the content and style. This is even more important if your child has
a significant problem with reading. Although he may only be able to read 'readers'
that a five-year old is reading, he will enjoy you reading a novel that is more
appropriate for a seven-year old.

Adeney, Anne, 1998, *I Have a Plan*, Orion Publishing Group, London, UK.
Blyton, Enid, 1991, *The Famous Five* series, Hodder Children's Books, London, UK.
Dahl, Roald, 1988, *Matilda*, Puffin Books, London, UK.
French, Jackie, 2001, *A Story to Eat with a Mandarin*, Angus&Robertson, Australia.
French, Jackie, 1999, *Stories to Eat with a Watermelon*, Angus&Robertson,
    Australia.
Hirsch, Odo, 1999, *Hazel Green*, Allen & Unwin, Australia.
Mitchell, Elyne, 1998, *A Brumby Story: Dancing Brumby's Rainbow*,
    Angus&Robertson, Australia.
Rodda, Emily, 2001, *Dog Tales,* Scholastic Australia.
Rowling, J.K., 1997, *Harry Potter and the Philosopher's Stone*, Bloomsbury
    Publishers, London, UK.
Rowling, J.K., 1998, *Harry Potter and the Chamber of Secrets*, Bloomsbury
    Publishers, London, UK.
Rowling, J.K., 1999, *Harry Potter and the Prisoner of Azkaban*, Bloomsbury
    Publishers, London, UK.
Rowling, J.K., 2000, *Harry Potter and the Goblet of Fire*, Bloomsbury Publishers,
    London, UK.
White, E.B., 1963, *Charlotte's Web*, Puffin Books, London, UK.

Futher reading for parents and carers

Reading and literacy

Butler, Dorothy, 1980, *Babies Need Books*, Atheneum, USA.

Dewsbury, Alison, 1995, *First Steps, Parents as Partners: Helping your Child's Literacy and Language Development*, Longman Australia.

Doman, Glenn, 2002, *How to Teach Your Baby to Read,* Pan Books, USA.

Engleman, Siegfried, 1986, *Teach Your Child to Read*, Simon & Schuster, USA.

Fox, Mem, 2001, *Reading Magic*, Pan Macmillan Australia.

Gillert, S. & Bernhardt, M.1988, *Reading Rescue*, Australian Council for Educational Research, Australia.

Moloney, James, 2001, *Boys and Books*, ABC Books, Sydney, Australia.

Owocki, Gretchen, 1999, *Literacy through Play*, Heinemann, UK.

Rief, Sandra, 2001, *Ready Start School*, Prentice Hall. New Jersey, USA.

Roskos, K. et al., 2000, *Play and Literacy in Early Childhood: Research from Multiple Perspectives*, Lawrence Erlbaum Association, New Jersey, USA.

Self-help and special needs

Attwood, Tony, 1998, *Asperger's Syndrome: A Guide for Parents and Professionals*, Jessica Kingsley Pub, London, UK.

Biddulph, S., 1993, *The Secret of Happy Children*, Bay Books, Australia.

Biddulph, S., 1997, *Raising Boys, Finch Publishing*, Sydney, Australia.

Covey, Stephen, 1998, *The 7 Habits of Highly Effective Families*, Allen & Unwin, Sydney, Australia.

Cryer, Debby et al, 1987, *Active Learning for Infants / Ones / Twos / Threes*, Addison Wesley Publishing Company, USA.

Cumine, Val et al., 1998, *Asperger's Syndrome: A Practical Guide for Teachers*, David Fulton Pub, London, UK.

Cumine, Val et al., 2000, *Autism in the Early Years: A Practical Guide*, David Fulton Pub, London, UK.

Dinkmeyer, D. et al., 1997, *The Parent's Handbook: Systematic Training for Effective Parenting*, American Guidance Services, USA.

Dougherty, Dorothy et al., 2001, *How to Talk to Your Baby*, Avery/Putnam, USA.

Dunn, Kylie, 1997, *The Sound Sleuth*, Pearson Education Company, New Jersey, USA.

Dunn, Kylie, 1999, *Maths Magic*, Prim-Ed Publishing, UK.

Flick, Grad L., 1996, *Power Parenting for Children with ADD/ADHD*, Jossey-Bass, San Francisco.

Green, Christopher, 1994, *Understanding ADD*, Doubleday Books, Sydney, Australia.

Green, Dr C., 1985, *Toddler Taming: The Guide to Your Child From One to Four*, Doubleday, Australia.

Green, Dr C., 1994, *Babies*, Simon & Schuster, Australia.

Greenberg, S., et al., 1991, *Attention Deficit Hyperactivity Disorder, Questions and Answers for Parents*, Research Press, Illinois, USA.

Gregory, Sheila, 1986 , *First Fun*, Century Hutchinson, New Zealand.

Hammond, Lorraine, 1996, *When Bright Kids Fail*, Simon & Schuster, Australia.

Hornsby, Beve, 1984, *Overcoming Dyslexia: A Parents Survival Guide*, Methuen, UK.

Hornsby, Beve, 1988, *Overcoming Dyslexia*, Macdonald & Co Pub, UK.

Hornsby, Beve, 1997, *Alpha to Omega*, Heinemann Educational Books, UK.

Humphreys, Tony, 1993, *Self-Esteem: The Key to Your Child's Education*, Newleaf, Dublin, Ireland.

Jackson, Merrill, 1991, *Discipline: An Approach For Teachers and Parents*, Longman Cheshire, Australia.

Johnson, Spencer, 1983, *The One Minute Father, Colombus Books*, London.

Johnson, Spencer, 1985, *The One Minute Mother, Colombus Books*, London.

Karnes, Merle B., 1982, *You and Your Small Wonder*, American Guidance Services, USA.

Kuffner, Trish, 2000, *The Toddler's Busy Book*, Meadowbrook, Minnesotta, USA.

Levett, T. & Petersen, Linda, 2002, *Social Savvy*, Australian Council for Educational Research, Australia.

Lewis, Barbara, 2000, *Being Your Best: Character Building for Kids 7–10*, Free Spirit Publishing, Minneapolis, USA.

Matthews, Andrew, 1990, *Being Happy: A Handbook to Greater Confidence and Security*, Media Masters, New Zealand.

McAleer Hamaguchi, Patricia, 1995, *Childhood Speech, Language and Listening Problems: What Every Parent Should Know*, John Wiley & Sons, Australia.

Petersen,Lindy, 2002, *Stop and Think Learning*, Australian Council for Educational Research, Australia.

Petrie, Pat, 1987, *Baby Play*, Pantheon Books, USA.

Powers, Michael (ed.), 2000, *Children with Autism: A Parent's Guide*, Woodbine House, USA.

Rapee, Ronald et al., 2000, *Helping Your Anxious Child*, New Harbinger Pub, Oakland, California, USA.

Rickard, Jenny, 1996, *Relaxation for Children*, Collins Dove, Australia.

Rief, Sandra, 1993, *How to Reach and Teach ADD / ADHD Children*, Jossey-Bass, San Francisco, USA.

Sanders, Matthew, 1992, *Every Parent*, Addison-Wesley Publishing Company, Sydney.

Sears, William & Thompson, Lynda, 1998, *The ADD Book: New Understandings, New Approaches to Parenting Your Child*, Little, Brown & Co., Boston, USA.

Serfontein, Gordon, 1993, *The Hidden Handicap*, Simon & Schuster, USA.

Silberman, M & Wheelan, S., 1980, *How to Discipline without Feeling Guilty*, Research Press, Illinois.

Smith, Brenda et al., 1998, *Asperger's Syndrome: A Guide for Educators and Parents*, Pro-ed, Austin, Texas.

Stanley, I. & Greenspan, H. et al., 1998, *The Child with Special Needs*, Perseus Books, Massachusetts, USA.

Useful websites for parents and children

Net Nannies

These sites provide up-to-date information on filtering the content of Internet material for use by children:

www.crayoncrawler.com

www.netparents.org

www.safekids.com

www.youngmedia.org.au

Educational software

Broderbund Software Inc — www.broder.com

Compu Ed — www.compued.com.au

Disney Interactive — www.disneyinteractive.com

Earobics — www.cogcon.com

Edmark — www.edmark.com

Edsoft — www.edsoft.com.au

Greygum — www.greygum.com.au

Lego Media International — www.legomedia.com

Macro Works — www.eduss.com

New Horizons — www.nh.com.au

Scholastic — www.scholastic.com.au

Scientific Learning (Fast ForWord) — www.scilearn.com

Sherston — www.sherston.com

Spectronics — www.spectronicsinoz.com

The Learning Company — www.learningco.com

Some popular children's Internet sites

www.abc-read.com — Advice and activities for parents to use to help their child.

www.ajkids.com — A search engine that allows children to ask specific questions.

www.ala.org/ICONN/topten.html — Provides a list of the top ten sites for kids.

www.beritsbest.com — A range of activities from games to information and chat lines.

www.edna.edu.au — Accesses the Education Network Australia Directory, excellent for finding educational sites.

www.galaxykids.com.au — For Australian residents only; activities are brightly coloured, fun and interactive. However, after the free tour you will have to subscribe if you wish to participate in the weekly program.

www.ipl.org — An Internet Public Library site, offering a wealth of books and information as well as links to online bookshops.

www.kahootz.com — A secure website set up by the Australian Children's Television Foundation.

www.kidsdomain.com — Full of activities, entertainment, science etc, recommended software downloads by subject or age.

www.kidznet.au — You have to subscribe to this site, which then gives you access to thousands of recommended sites for children.

www.mamamedia.com — A fun site with children's games.

www.picturewordwall.com — A wide range of early reading resources and activities.

www.quia.com/dir/el/ — Activities and games for early learning.

www.waterfordpress.com/game1.html — An enormous number of free games and activities for young children.

www.zamaman.com.au — Educational downloads, online games and resources for parents and teachers.

Directory of speech and language therapy associations

National Office
2nd Floor
11–19 Bank Place
Melbourne 3000
Tel: 03 9642 4899
www.speechpathologyaustralia.org.au

New South Wales
PO Box 150
Concord NSW 2137
Tel: 02 9743 0013

Victoria
c/– National Office

ACT
GPO Box 1793
Civic ACT 2601

South Australia
42 Lorraine Avenue
Lockleys SA 5032
Tel: 08 8354 4738

Queensland
c/– The Glenleighden School
Cubberla Street
Fig Tree Pocket QLD 4069

Tasmania

PO Box 355

Moonah TAS 7892

Western Australia

1/37 Baldwin Street

Como WA 6152

Tel: 08 8950 8281

Northern Territory

PO Box 41328

Casuarina NT 0811

New Zealand

Speech-Language Therapist Association

Suite 369

63 Remeura Road

Newmarket Auckland NZ

Tel: 64 3 235 8257

Email: nzsta@clear.net.nz

Support groups

There are many support groups from around the world, including Australia, listed on the International Resource for Special Children website. This site provides articles and resources as well as chat lines. The address is www.irsc.org.

This wonderful site covers information about adaptive education and technologies, autistic spectrum disorders, Down's syndrome, communication disorders, hearing impaired, learning disabilities, associated issues of law, neurological problems, rare disorders and many more. It is an excellent site for professionals as well as parents and is very user-friendly.

Another fantastic web site is Dr Caroline Bowen's masterpiece. Dr Bowen is a Sydney-based speech and language pathologist who has put together an amazing collection of resources, links, support groups and information for both professionals and parents. You can access it at http://members.tripod.com/Caroline_Bowen /whatshere.htm or www.slpsite.com

Bibliography

Adams, C., 2001, 'Clinical Diagnostic Intervention Studies of Children with Pragmatic
Disorder', *International Journal of Language Communication Disorders*, Vol. 36, No. 3.

Arnberg, Lenore, 1987, *Raising Children Bilingually, Multilingual Matters,* Avon, UK.

Australian Bureau of Statistics, 2001, *What kids get up to.*

Ayres, Jean, 1972, *Sensory Integration and Learning Disorders*, Western Psychological
Services, Los Angeles, California, USA.

Ayres, Jean, 1979, *Sensory Integration and the Child*, Western Psychological Services,
Los Angeles, California, USA.

Bishop, Dorothy (ed), 1993, *Language Development in Exceptional Circumstances*,
Churchill Livingstone, Edinburgh, UK.

Bochner, Sandra, Price, Penny & Salamon, Linda, 1988, *Learning to Talk*, Macquarie
University, Sydney, Australia.

Broomfield, Hilary & Combley, Margaret, 1997, *Overcoming Dyslexia*, Whurr
Publishers, London, UK.

Cooper, Carol, 1997, *Twins & Multiple Birth: The Essential Parenting Guide from
Birth to Adulthood*, Vermilion/Random House, UK.

Fernando, Carmen, 1998, *Tongue Tie: From Confusion to Clarity*, Tandem Publications, Sydney, Australia

Fey, Marc, 1986, *Language Intervention with Young Children*, Pro-ed, Austin, Texas.

Fox, A. V., Dodd, B, & Howard, D., 2002, 'Risk Factors for Speech Disorders in Children', *International Journal of Language Communication Disorders*, Vol. 37, No. 2.

Goleman, Daniel, 1995, *Emotional Intelligence*, Bantam Books, New York, USA.

Hammer, C. S., Tombin, J. B., Zhang, X. & Weiss, A., 2001, 'Relationship between Parenting Behaviours and Specific Language Impairment in Children', *International Journal of Language Communication Disorders*, Vol. 36, No. 2.

Kilminster & Laird, 1978, 'Articulation Development in Children Aged Three to Nine Years', *Australian Journal of Human Communication Disorder*, Vol. 6, No. 1.

Langrehr, John, 1999, *Teaching Your Child to Think*, Wrightbooks Pty Ltd., Victoria, Australia.

Law, J. et al., 2000, 'Prevalence and Natural History of Primary Speech and Language Delay', *International Journal of Language and Communication Disorders*, Vol. 35, No. 2.

Luke, Carmen, 1988, *TV and Your Child*, Kagan and Woo, Canada.

Manolson, Ayala, 1992, *It Takes Two to Talk*, A Hanen Centre Publication, Toronto, Canada.

Menyuk, Paula, 1988, *Language Development*, Longman Publishers, USA.

Pratt, Chris & Garton, Alison, 1998, *Learning to be Literate: The Development of Spoken and Written Language*, Blackwell Publishers, Oxford, UK.

Snowling, M. & Stackhouse, J., 1997, *Dyslexia: Speech and Language*, Whurr Publishers, London, UK.

Snowling, M., 1997, *Academic Success*, Whurr Publishers, London, UK.

Snowling, M., Adams, J., Bishop, D. & Stothard, E., 2001, 'Educational Attainments of School Leavers with a Preschool History of Speech and Language Impairment', *International Journal of Speech and Communication Disorders*, Vol. 36, No. 36.

Van Norman, R., 1999, *Helping the Thumb Sucking Child: A Practical Guide for Parents*, Avery Penguin Putnam, New York, USA.

Wallach, G. & Miller, L., 1988, *Language Intervention and Academic Success*, Little, Brown and Co., Boston, USA.

Wiener, Harvey S., 1988, *Talk with Your Child*, Penguin Books, Virginia, USA.

Wood, David J., 1998, *How Children Think and Learn: The Social Context of Cognitive Development*, Blackwell Publishers, Oxford, UK.

Yule, George, 2002, *The Study of Language*, Cambridge University, Press, Cambridge, UK.

Index